ISLANDS
for
DISCOVERY

An Outdoors Guide to B.C.'s
Queen Charlotte Islands

Dennis Horwood & Tom Parkin

Foreword by R.D. Lawrence

Orca Book Publishers

Second printing 1990
Third printing 1991
Fourth printing 1994

Canadian Cataloguing in Publication Data

Horwood, Dennis, 1951-
  Islands for discovery

  Bibliography: p.
  Includes index.

ISBN 0-920501-23-0

  1. Natural history — British Columbia — Queen Charlotte Islands — Guide-books. 2. Queen Charlotte Islands (B.C.) — Description and travel — Guide-books. I. Parkin, Tom, 1953- II. Title.
QH106.2.B7H67 1989   508.711'31   C89-091236-X

Orca Book Publishers Ltd.
P.O. Box 5626, Stn. B
Victoria, B.C., Canada
V8R 6S4

Orca Book Publishers Ltd.
P.O. Box 468
Custer, WA. USA
98240-0468

Cover design by Susan Fergusson

Photographs by the authors except as otherwise noted.

Typeset by AMS Graphics, Victoria, B.C.
Printed in Canada by Hignell Printing Ltd., Winnipeg, Manitoba.

To our enthusiastic and supportive field companions,
Brenda Horwood and Doug Eastcott.

Acknowledgements

The production of this book involved the effort of many people whose names do not appear on the cover. We have relied on the research of other authors and critical review of our text by many authorities. While accepting final responsibility for any errors, we'd like to thank:

Kathryn Bernick, Bill Holm of the Burke Museum at the University of Washington, as well as Kevin Neary and Dr. Jim Haggarty of the Royal B.C. Museum for their suggestions for improvements in the archeology sections; Drs. Michael Bigg and Jim Darling as well as Don Blood for their marine mammal comments; Michael Brown, Mrs. Janet Gifford-Brown, Rick Howie, John Woods, and Steven McConnell for bird observations; Sheila Charneski, Rosemary and Ken Maitland, and Peter Kalina for proof-reading and finding fuzzy expression; Dr. John Clague of the Geological Survey of Canada for ensuring accuracy in Naikoon Park sedimentology, Supervisor Earl Coatta and Norman Dressler of the Atmospheric Environment Service of Canada for updating climatic information; Doug Eastcott and Stephen Suddes of the Canadian Parks Service for keeping us abreast of developments in the South Moresby Reserve; Ted Griff for his computer expertise; James Dawes and Rick Heathman of B.C. Provincial Parks for style suggestions and for checking the Naikoon Park chapters; Brenda Horwood for expediting services and proof-reading; Captain David Littlejohn for marine advice; Dugald Nasmith of Pacific Rim Paddling Company for culinary and guiding services; Dr. Wayne Nelson of the University of Calgary for details on Langara Island; Dr. Jim Pojar, Ministry of Forests, and Kerry Joy of B.C. Parks for identifying plant photos and checking the rainforest chapter; Dr. Hans Roemer and John Pinder-Moss of the B.C. Ecological Reserves Program; Tom Rutherford and Richard Thomson, Department of Fisheries and Oceans, for sharing their knowledge of fisheries and oceanography; and finally Doug Steventon and Steve Aitkins for providing interesting local detail.

We thank publisher Bob Tyrrell for his recognition of the need for this book (may it be long-lived!), and for his guidance through the necessary rewrites.

Finally, Curator Wayne Campbell of the Royal B.C. Museum was outstanding for his encouragement, collation of wildlife records, and constructive comments on the entire manuscript.

Contents

Foreword

When I heard from Tom Parkin that he and Dennis Horwood had co-authored a book describing the rich beauty of the Queen Charlotte Islands, I was pleased. At last, I said to myself, somebody has done pictorial and literary justice to these magnificent islands. When I realized that his letter went on to ask if I would write this foreword, I was delighted. *Islands for Discovery* is an apt title for a guide book that presents for its readers the geography, natural history, and history of the Queen Charlotte Islands, for nobody can visit Canada's westernmost, sea-lapped shores without being immediately confronted with a variety of discoveries. And that's even *before* landing from a vessel — a form of transport that, in my view, is the very best way to travel to the islands.

To my everlasting regret, I have only paid two visits to the Charlottes, appetite-whetting trips that ended all too soon. Because of this lack, I have for years longed for a book that would offer me an intimate look at the land, its people, and its biology. Now my longing has been well satisfied.

When I first set out to write this foreword, I thought that I might start by describing the scenery, the wave-battered, fascinating coves and bays, the huge, majestic evergreens, and the marine and land life. In the end I realized that such description would be redundant. Parkin and Horwood have done the job already; and they have done it far better than ever I could, for they know their turf, and, it is clear, they have a great love for it.

Writers of forewords can all too easily fall in love with their own prose and become boring. I do not want to do that. *Islands for Discovery* is too interesting and its readers do not deserve to be held up by me. They should, instead, be allowed to enter its pages as quickly as possible.

A book as good as this one *ought* to have been produced a long time ago. But, never mind, it is here now. Read it ! I know that you will enjoy it.

R. D. Lawrence
Haliburton Highlands
Ontario

9

ISLANDS
for
DISCOVERY

I. Background Information

Introduction

The geographical area known as the Queen Charlotte Islands is made up of a tight cluster of islands which lie 50 to 150 kilometres (31 to 95 miles) off the northwestern coast of British Columbia. Once thought of as remote and largely isolated even from the rest of Canada, recent developments have made Canadians and others throughout the world aware of this very special and beautiful area. During the 1970s an ongoing series of articles, books, and television programs began to publicize the exceptional nature of the environment of the Queen Charlotte Islands, and the people who live there. Events focusing on the land claims of native people, the creation of a national park reserve and the struggle for the protection of the environment during the 1980s have continued to promote awareness of the islands both nationally and internationally. So much so that by 1988 a Ministry of Tourism survey found that three out of four visitors to British Columbia expressed a desire to visit the Queen Charlotte Islands. Though summer tourism has increased enormously since regular ferry service was initiated in 1980, the Islands still have relatively few visitors. Other places in B.C. known for their scenery and sophistication continue to draw most tourists who visit the province. Those who do visit the Queen Charlottes tend to be adventure-oriented, recreation-focused, and aware of the natural environment. They also spend more time on their visit than do tourists to other locales; they seem to seek to understand the Charlottes, and they often come away with profound appreciation of their experience. This book is for them.

There are roughly 150 islands in the Queen Charlotte archipelago, and they form a shape not unlike a scimitar. The largest island, Graham, is the curving blade. A narrow but navigable channel separates it from its handle, Moresby Island, on the south. Smaller Langara, Louise, Lyell, Burnaby, and Kunghit islands are like

11

encrusting jewels. The total land area of the archipelago is approximately 9940 square km (3976 sq mi). This is much smaller than Vancouver Island, B.C.'s largest island, but seventy-five percent larger than Prince Edward Island, Canada's smallest province.

The Charlottes, as they're known for short, rise near the outer edge of the continental shelf. A shallow inshore water body called Hecate Strait separates the islands from the mainland. Dixon Entrance is a heaving gap of ocean lying between the Queen Charlotte Islands and the islands to the north which form the Alaskan panhandle. Vancouver Island is 240 km (150 mi) to the south. Although Canada's coast includes thousands of islands, the Charlottes are the most isolated.

The Queen Charlotte Islands contain a wide variety of landscapes. Geologist A. Sutherland Brown states that they are like a model of B.C. because most types of terrain present elsewhere in the province are represented here in miniature. There are broad beaches of sand and columns of sandstone, there are sea-carved caves and cliffs of volcanic bedrock, there are sediments of glaciation, and there are strata famous for their fossils.

The Queen Charlotte Mountains, a ridge of rugged and steep terrain frequently incised by straits and fjords, form a divide along the western edge of Graham and Moresby islands. The surf-smashed west coast, wide open to North Pacific winds, is probably the highest-energy coast in the country. Unfortunately the general inaccessibility means that this beautiful area is infrequently visited. Moresby Island is generally narrow with steep slopes and few lakes, but Graham has rolling plateaus and muskeg lowlands on its eastern side. The heart of Graham is washed by salt water through Masset Inlet, "the lake" to the locals. Freshwater streams and rivers everywhere are short but numerous.

Over all of this scrambles verdant vegetation with a greater density of living matter than tropical jungles. The giant conifers of the Charlottes are unexcelled in height and grandeur by any forest in Canada. These cedar, spruce, and hemlock trees are among the best examples of temperate rainforest found in North America, and were essential in the development of the aboriginal culture. In 1988 some stands were assured of perpetuity by the designation of a national park reserve.

These magnificent conifers are also the chief measure of commerce on the islands. The forest industry is the greatest single employer in the Charlottes. Often, and quite understandably, the reservation of lands for conservation purposes doesn't sit well with those whose livelihood depends on the harvesting of the forests. Fortunately, however, many residents are beginning to understand the long-term importance of conservation and careful land management. Still, islanders find little full-time employment in a region which otherwise offers only commercial fishing and the infrequent mining job. None of these resources are processed here, and government and the tourism service industry have previously offered only minor opportunities. Tourism offers perhaps the greatest potential for the future of the economy of the Queen Charlotte Islands. In the past the tourist industry was based largely on sport fishing. Recent developments, however, suggest the potential for considerable expansion and diversification as the world comes to investigate rumours of this seabound Shangri-la.

European discovery of the Charlottes was first recorded by the Spaniard Juan Perez in 1774. Although he never went ashore, Perez did encounter a group of Haida who came out to greet his ship in dugout canoes. Other navigators from New Spain (now California) ventured into the region in 1775 and 1779.

Although the great British captain, Cook, missed the islands altogether on his trip up the coast in 1778, he did pick up sea otter pelts in Alaska which eventually sold in China for an astronomical sum. Thus started the maritime fur trade which was to annihilate all the sea otters in the Charlottes, and nearly extinguished the species. By 1786 British ships direct from England, the Orient, and India were competing to trade with natives all along the Pacific Northwest coast. Captain George Dixon visited the Charlottes that year, and was the first to discover that the islands were insular. It was he who named them after his ship and sovereign — Queen Charlotte.

The islands eventually became trading territory for Americans as well. Unfortunately the aggressive attitude of these efficient competitors had serious consequences for both the Haida and other traders. The intimidation and force used by Captain Robert Gray initiated a series of violent attacks by the natives, who believed in vicarious responsibility. As the sea otter population declined, trade methods became more ruthless. There was murder on both sides.

More settled policies were re-introduced when the British traders of the Hudson's Bay Company began construction of permanent trading posts on the north coast in 1831. The HBC restricted the sale of firearms, ammunition, and liquor. Although this lowered their profits, it resulted in a good deal more stability. With the British establishing colonies on the south coast, and the Russians firmly in control of the north, the Americans eventually quit the territory.

Unfortunately for the Haida, the introduction of Western civilization was not at all to their benefit. Contagious disease, illegal alcohol, poverty, and in-fighting slowly destroyed what had been one of the strongest native cultures on the coast. Concerned religious societies sent out missionaries to control the demoralization and convert the heathen. These preachers eventually wielded enormous influence, and introduced further change into native social patterns. The Haida eventually made the transition to a new way of life, but the consequences were a further deterioration in their culture, pride, and people. This was a sad period for a region which once had the highest population density in North America. At their lowest ebb in 1915, Haida numbers had declined ninety percent from pre-contact times.

The early post-contact history of the islands followed a fairly typical pattern and was characterized by the usual retinue of missionaries, resource developers and homesteaders. But nothing came easy in this rugged and isolated environment. Certainly the churches made lasting inroads in their search for souls and the lumber industry has managed to survive; few homesteaders, however, found the climate hospitable to their needs. The history of the Charlottes has been well-documented in several books mentioned in the **Further Reading** section.

About 6000 Canadians of many descents live on the Charlottes today. Like islanders everywhere, they enjoy their isolation and lifestyle and are often resistant to change. They're particularly interested in maintaining local control over developments which influence their lives. You'll find they prefer a certain amount of challenge over modern convenience.

Although Islanders frequently demonstrate the manana attitude, don't be fooled into thinking these are backwater folks. Many are very talented; lots are jacks-of-all-trades since work and supplies are so often expensive or in short supply. The success of people here is rarely measured on a financial scale; personal accomplishment and individuality seem much more important factors than simple monetary success. As a result you'll find high levels of confidence and personality among the locals. 'Characters' tend to develop or be nourished in this environment. Don't be surprised when you hear monikers such as Sid the Wrench, Huckleberry, or Stickleback Tom. Time spent meeting the people of the Queen Charlottes will provide as many memorable moments as the spectacular landscape.

Accommodation and Camping

Overnight facilities on the islands range from modern hotels to homes with 'bag and breakfast' for backpackers. The most reliable method of choosing a place to sleep is to obtain the annual *Accommodation Guide* published by the B.C. Ministry of Tourism. It lists businesses which meet reasonable standards, but excludes bed and breakfast places. Such approved facilities will display a blue sign or decal near their entrance. The *Accommodation Guide* is available for free from over 140 Travel Infocentres located throughout the province or from:

> Tourism British Columbia
> 1117 Wharf Street
> Victoria, B.C. V8W 2Z2
> Telephone: 1-800-663-6000 (U.S. or Canada)

These offices can also supply *Outdoor and Adventure Vacations*, a free catalogue of adventure resorts and tours for the province, including some on the Queen Charlotte Islands.

Campgrounds on the Charlottes are generally simple; in 1988 only two, in Masset and in Sandspit, had hook-ups for RVs. The Canadian Parks Service expects to start construction of a campground at Gordon Cove on Cumshewa Inlet in 1989. At the moment the B.C. government provides two serviced campsites in Naikoon Provincial Park. There is a user fee for them, and reservations are not accepted. The *Accommodation Guide* lists private campsites that are approved. Free primitive campsites are located in various backroad locations. The **Communities** section of this chapter and site-specific chapters later mention campsites near places to explore.

Camping within any Indian reserve is prohibited by the Haida. In other locations you can camp anywhere on provincial crown land. Look for beaches along the east coast or beside rivers along backroads. At the beach, be cautious of setting fires near the driftwood. Winds can create an ugly conflagration if you leave your fire untended. In all uncontrolled places, remove your garbage and bury sewage deeply. These islands will stay beautiful because you care.

For tenters, a wind-proof and water-proof design with a fly is necessary. In wet weather you'll be miserably confined in anything flimsy. In addition, every campsite will benefit from a tarp to keep rain off the cooking area or to provide a windbreak.

Chartering and Tours

Visitors without boats who want to see backcountry waters must hire a plane or boat with an operator to take them there. Even if you are kayaking, a one-way charter can double your time in new areas. Split amongst a party, chartering costs are relatively low for the lengthened field experience they allow. The procedure isn't difficult, and this section will enable you to obtain the best value for your needs.

Airplanes in the Charlottes use both land and water. The size of plane needed is determined by the weight and size of your party. When chartering, you are renting both the machine and pilot, so rates aren't determined by the number of seats occupied. The cost will be determined by either an hourly or distance rate. Sometimes fuel cost is factored in, other times it's an additional charge. There will also be minor charges for additional landings en route to your final destination. Estimates are freely given by companies beforehand. Don't forget that you will also pay for the plane's return to base.

Unlike scheduled airlines, flying by charter is susceptible to passenger and weather delays. You may have to wait for other bookings to be transported before your group can depart, so it's always best to make reservations so that carriers will space their parties accordingly. If problems prevent your pick-up at a specified time, don't leave your location. Delays will rarely be more than forty-eight hours. But be prepared. Every party should carry extra food for such a contingency.

Your pilot has the final say as to where he beaches, and does the loading. Gasoline must be carried in approved containers, and outboard motors must be drained of fuel since altitude changes may cause vaporization into the cabin. One canoe or kayak less than 5.1 metres (17 ft) long can be tied externally on planes such as Beavers and Otters if wind and insurance conditions permit. There will be a surcharge for this, and passengers may have to travel separately.

Unloading a Grumman Goose on Hotspring Island. Vintage WW II, these amphibious war horses are able to take off and land on water or airstrips.

The three most common airplanes available in the Charlottes are: the de Havilland Beaver, the de Havilland single-engine Otter, and the Grumman Goose. Though old, these are the classic bush planes which opened up the Canadian coast and territories. Beavers can carry 360 kilograms (800 pounds) or four passengers, Otters can carry 720 kg (1600 lbs) or eight passengers, the Goose can carry 810 kg (1800 lbs) or nine passengers. We have successfully flown a Goose packed with six passengers, three double collapsible kayaks, and gear for a two-week expedition.

Helicopters can't carry such loads, but will take you into places fixed-wings can't land. The rotary-wings are chartered on an hourly rate, but time is calculated on in-air time only. There is normally no standby charge unless you cause a lengthy wait during the busy summer. Some of the companies at Sandspit have set tour itineraries and prices. Safety is emphasized in helicopter operation. Your pilot will brief you on the basics, then provide verbal and hand signals for approaching and leaving the aircraft. And what a great way to fly!

Boats are another consideration. Chartering a boat to go fishing for the day is a relatively simple and safe venture. Several local people specialize in this activity. However, if you decide to charter a local boat to take you on an extended tour, you would be well advised to proceed with caution. Marine touring is a fledgling industry for these operators. For the most part they have not as yet gained the expertise of captains from southern ports who operate specialized tours in these waters from May to September. Obviously, as business picks up, this is an area that will improve.

Still, forewarned is forearmed. Shop around. Inspect your prospective vessel beforehand, noting safety equipment and level of maintenance. Ask the vessel owner how long he's been in business and whether he has knowledge of the places you intend to visit or your particular interests. For example, only one local vessel caters specifically to scuba divers. Ask whether food costs are included, who prepares the meals, and what kind of menu can be expected. Find out where you can go ashore, whether anyone else will be along, and whether the owner has time constraints. Know whether the charter is covered by insurance, and under what conditions refunds are given. We speak from bitter experience!

Many of these same inquiries will help you select a capable tour group if you are letting someone else do the organizing. Always obtain a company's literature before booking. In addition to the questions above, ask what their guide-to-participant ratio is, and how large the trip will be. Few local tour operators advertise off-island, so you may be able to meet the people involved.

Climate and Clothing

The climate in the Charlottes is widely variable. The Queen Charlotte Mountains attain elevations of 1050 m (3500 ft), high enough to wrestle with tumultuous storm clouds driven by offshore winds. Coastal areas near the mountains can be particularly windy and wet. Yet just a few kilometres inland conditions can change considerably. The winds can taper off, the air temperature rise, and the rainfall can be significantly reduced. This rainshadow effect is most noticeable on Graham Island. It disappears where the land narrows toward southern Moresby Island. Less than one percent of Canada feels this unusual blend of oceanic storms, cloudy skies, cool summers, and relatively mild wet winters.

Overall, weather on the islands has two patterns. From mid-May until September winds blow most frequently from the northwest. By late September a new system begins to form in the Gulf of Alaska, and wind arrives from the southeast for the rest of the winter. Storms are worst from October to January, and are repetitive. Cape St. James bears the brunt of this force, and is the windiest place recorded in Canada. Wind speed here is 33.7 kilometres per hour (21.2 mph), averaged over twenty-six years. Of course the wind has less strength inland. 'Southeasters' bring rain and calmer water — good fishing weather.

While the Misty Isles justify their name, recreationists should come prepared for sunburn as well. By a wide margin, May is the month with the highest average hours of sunshine.

The mountains influence other island climate patterns as well. Rainfall measurements here have not set national records, but they are impressive. The average annual precipitation of 4218 millimetres (169 inches) at Tasu on the west coast compares favourably with other places on B.C.'s coast with reputations for high rainfall. October is the wettest month, and the west coast is the wettest location on these islands. The same mountains which force clouds to drop their precipitation shield the lee of the islands. East coast communities receive only an average 1100 to 1300 mm (44 to 52 in) annually. May, June, and July are the driest months, and Tlell and Sandspit are the driest places on the islands. They get the same amount of summer precipitation as do the prairie provinces of Canada.

Tlell and Sandspit are also the warmest towns on the islands. Days of 32° Centigrade (89° Fahrenheit) have been recorded, but you can expect daytime temperatures in August (the warmest month) of around 17° C (62° F) throughout the islands. That isn't particularly warm for summer, but then it isn't particularly cold here in winter either. January is the coldest month, and even then daytime temperatures usually rise above freezing. The moderating influence of the ocean ensures upwards of two hundred frost-free days each year near the water. This combination of a cool water body and warm air frequently creates fog which gives the Charlottes their romantic name, "The Misty Isles."

There can be snow, but it typically doesn't last long at lower elevations. The mountains do get lots of the white stuff, and it can take most of the summer to melt a heavy snowpack above the 750 m (2500 ft) level.

Wind is the greatest hazard to water travellers. Winds can come up suddenly, blow vigorously, and may not die for days. Even within the protected channels of Moresby Island, small boaters will need to plan contingent days for being weather-bound.

We strongly advise purchasing an economical pocket-sized weather receiver (available in many electronics shops). It will pick up continuous VHF weather reports broadcast by the Coast Guard. Mountain-top repeaters provide reception to most locations. If not, a small antenna held aloft on a paddle or oar significantly improves the reception. Alternately, you can carry an altimeter, which is simply a barometer which indicates changes in atmospheric pressure. It will provide some advance warning of worsening weather. The rule of marine survival is: obtain the latest weather information, and be prepared for anything.

Being prepared includes carrying gear for almost any condition. This doesn't mean an extra suitcase of clothes, simply a selection suited to your intended activities. Anyone getting in and out of small boats (even on organized yacht tours) will appreciate tall rubber boots. Sneakers are fine for walking on North Beach, though East Beach hikers require better ankle support.

Raingear is important even during the dry months. The quality of equipment depends on what you will be doing. Umbrellas are useless at any time of year in the Charlottes; use two-piece raingear. The breathable fabric Gortex doesn't perform well in the marine environment as salt clogs its pores. It will be okay for shore walks, but anyone fishing at sea will need coated fabrics with sealed seams. A sou'wester hat is great for the head, but a jacket hood pulled over a visored cap will suffice.

A toque will keep your head warm on overcast windy days, and a sweater is always useful under a windbreaker. Synthetic underwear and pile jackets are very popular as they retain warmth even if wet. Material such as denim dries slowly and isn't practical for the outdoors. And finally, do bring a bathing suit for swims at Pure Lake Park (Graham Island's swimmin' hole), and for soaks at Hotspring Island.

Communities and Facilities

Seven main communities dot the islands today, along with several logging camps and a number of former townsites which have retained a few occupants. From north to south, Graham Island has

Anyone contemplating an outdoor trip in the Charlottes needs to bring several changes of clothing, and take the earliest opportunity to dry out.

active villages at Haida, Masset, Port Clements, Tlell, Skidegate, Skidegate Landing and Queen Charlotte City.

Masset is the largest village. People there are primarily employed by the Canadian Armed Forces at a satellite tracking station called 'The Circle'. Its operations are a military semi-secret, and located underground except for a ring of towers and wires. Commercial fishing is also of importance here. Port Clements ('Port' for short) combines fishing with logging. Tlell is little more than a name on the map, but has an interesting assembly of artisans and small ranchers. Queen Charlotte City seems to have given up growth aspirations and is simply dubbed 'Charlotte'. Its central location and government offices have made it the unofficial capital of the islands.

Sandspit on Moresby Island contests this supremacy because it has the only airport, the most modern hotel, and is actively supported by the logging industry. The federal government small boat harbour and information centre planned in support of the new national park will provide it with additional advantage. But for the time being, Graham Island attracts most tourists.

Natives make up a minor portion of the island population. The aboriginal people have concentrated in two reserves called Haida and Skidegate. Haida, formerly Old Massett, was renamed to distinguish it from the adjacent white community of Masset. For similar reasons, off-reserve residents at Skidegate Landing have distinguished their locale adjacent to Skidegate with an additional word.

The major communities are located in this north-south line:

21

Masset facilities:

Scheduled seaplane service daily
Vehicle rentals and taxi service
Marine and automotive fuels, parts and service
Government pier and floats
Boat ramp at seaplane base
Motel, cabin and B&B accommodation
RV park with showers and five hookups (seasonal)
Sani-dump at seasonal Travel Infocentre
Restaurants, pub and grocery stores
Laundromat, pharmacy, liquor store, credit union
Hospital and public health nurse
Royal Canadian Mounted Police
18 hole golf course
Fishing guides, licences and tackle
Other stores and services

Port Clements facilities:

Automotive fuels and parts
Government pier and float, boat ramp
Motel with laundromat
Municipal campground and sani-station
Grocery store with liquor sales
Licensed restaurant and pub
Sporting goods store with licences
Water taxi service

Tlell facilities:

Provincial park campground and headquarters
Lodge accommodation

Skidegate area facilities:

Scheduled daily floatplane and ferry service
Water and road taxi service
Boat ramp and boat charters
Marine and automotive fuels and repair
Sleeping accommodation
Restaurant
Marine and fishing supplies, licences
General store
Travel Infocentre

Charlotte facilities:

Vehicle rentals and taxi service
Automotive fuels, parts, and service
Government wharf and floats
Hotel, motel, B&B, and sleeping accommodation
Campground without water or hookups
Restaurants and grocery stores
Laundromat, pharmacy, liquor store, credit union
Hospital and public health nurse
Royal Canadian Mounted Police
Boat charters and rentals
Other stores and services
MacMillan Bloedel Ltd. shops
Provincial and federal government offices

Sandspit facilities:

Paved airport with scheduled daily flights
Helicopter and seaplane charters
Vehicle rentals, fuels, and parts
Marine fuel available by truck only
Government pier (no floats) and boat ramp
Hotel, motel, lodge, and B&B accommodation
RV park with sani-dump and some hookups
Restaurants and lounge
Grocery stores, one with liquor sales
Outdoor supplies and licences
Hunting and fishing guides
18 hole golf course
Fletcher Challenge Canada office
Other stores and services

If you're not travelling on the Charlottes by organized tour, you should make as much advance preparation as possible. While most things you might want to purchase are available, prices are naturally higher. We caution against expecting mainland standards. Local businesses are not completely used to the demands of the tourism industry. Their quality levels are sometimes lower and service may be slower. Many people operate part-time from their homes or rely on word-of-mouth advertising.

The tourism agencies below will supply general information and brochures, but cannot make bookings. When in doubt, ask —

people are very approachable. In fact, make it a habit. Few attractions have signs — everybody here knows where things are!

For further information, contact:

Q.C. Islands Chamber of Commerce
Box 38
Masset, B.C. V0T lM0
Telephone: (604) 626-5211

or: North by Northwest Tourism Assn.
Box 1030
Smithers, B.C. VOJ 2NO
Telephone: (604) 847-5227

or: Joy La Fortune
Travel Infocentre
Box 337
Queen Charlotte City, B.C. V0T 1S0
Telephone: (604) 559-4742

Fishing

The primary protein source of islanders has long been the sea, for it provides everything fresher than can arrive by boat. The rod and reel recreation available on these islands is renowned since access is easy and the fish abundant.

Fishing can be divided into lake, stream, and saltwater activity. Steelhead and salmon are of greatest interest to anglers, but there are rainbow and cutthroat trout and Dolly Varden char in most streams and lakes as well. Many of these fish travel to sea. Small trailered boats can be launched on Mayer Lake in Naikoon Park and Mosquito and Skidegate Lakes on Moresby Island. The latter offer trout to 1.4 kg (3 lb) and Dolly Varden of 0.5 kg (1 lb). Only a few rivers can be drifted for short distances by boat due to logjams.

Former U.S. President Jimmy Carter includes a chapter on his Moresby fishing experiences in his book *An Outdoor Journal*. He states that his steelhead experiences here were among the best in North America. The season for these fighting fish starts in November, climaxes during the Christmas holidays, then declines toward spring. However, the timing of the runs varies somewhat from river to river. Note that some rivers have angling closures starting February 1st. Techniques vary according to the angler and the nature of the water. Among the best producers we later mention the Yakoun and Tlell rivers, and Pallant Creek.

Mid-September is when coho salmon aficionados arrive for stream fishing, so accommodation and vehicle rentals can be scarce at that time of year. Coho return to fresh water when fall rains raise the river levels enough to allow the fish in from the ocean to spawn. Good water includes the Tlell, Yakoun, Copper, and Deena Rivers. Since their stream gradients are low, they have tidal action as much as a kilometre (0.6 mi) inland. Check for triangular markers indicating the boundary of tidal fishing. Here, as throughout B.C., separate fishing licences are required for salt and fresh water. Licences and regulations may be obtained from the Government Agent in Queen Charlotte City or sporting goods merchants. The latter are listed under **Communities**. For the time being, no additional licence is necessary to fish in South Moresby National Park Reserve. National Park fishing licenses will be required when the B.C. government actually transfers the reserve lands to the federal government.

Saltwater fishing goes year round if you can tolerate the winter weather. We mention specific locale details in chapters on Tow Hill, Langara Island, Louise Island, and Skidegate Inlet. There is great fishing for salmon and bottomfish in many other locations as well. Bottom fish include halibut (easily as desirable as salmon from a culinary point of view), ling cod, and red snapper. These species can be caught by jigging on simple handlines, though you have to know what you are doing to land a large halibut. Popular lures include Reef Raiders and Buzz Bombs. However, bottomfish aren't always easily caught. Counting on fish for an expedition menu has meant going hungry for more than one intrepid traveller.

In the last five years several floating lodges, roaming ships, and one land lodge have attracted fly-in clients for saltwater fishing trips of up to five days. Most of these fancy facilities are on the west and north coast of Graham Island. Coho and spring salmon are their major attractions, but halibut are also sought. All trip bookings must be made in advance through offices in Victoria or the Vancouver area. Request a free copy of *Saltwater Fishing Guide* from Tourism B.C. (address above) for their locations. Inquire locally for the names of people who have smaller boats available for casual charter fishing.

If you don't have a boat, and your budget doesn't allow hiring accommodations or a guide, you still might catch saltwater fish

Only kayaks and inflatable boats are easy to launch at
Gray Bay. This area is within the fishing boundaries of
the annual Sandspit coho derby each September.

from shore. Surf casters have brought in halibut from the rocks at
the foot of Tow Hill in Naikoon Park, though there's an equal
chance of catching spiny dogfish, a small undesirable shark. Other
anglers report success with young coho and pink salmon from the
spit at Sandspit, and south-side beaches in Skidegate Inlet, and in
Rennell Sound.

Once spawning starts, salmon concentrate at the mouths of their
home streams. Thus on the four September weekends each year the
Sandspit Rod and Gun Club sponsors a coho derby. To be eligible,
fish must be caught between Gray Bay and the Deena River on
Moresby Island. The coho, though much smaller than the spring
(also called king or chinook) salmon, has a reputation as the wildest
fighter of the salmonid family. A fish in the 3 - 5 kg (6 - 12 lb) range
can provide tremendous excitement when caught on light tackle.
Many anglers concentrate on the Copper River estuary where a
sizable encampment of the devoted suddenly appears during the
derby. This competition is open to visitors and residents alike, and
prizes are awarded in various categories. The largest coho caught is
usually in the 9 kg (20 lb) range.

Finally, saltwater fishing includes shellfish and crab harvesting.
No licence is required for these species. However, the islands are
under a permanent bivalve closure due to paralyzing toxins found in
molluscs. Abalone and razor clams don't accumulate this poison, so
may be harvested within the limits. Shrimp, prawns, and crabs
aren't affected either. Dungeness crabs are the favourite (should we
say flavourite?) A collapsible crab trap baited with any smelly scrap

or tinned meat or fish should produce a cracking good meal off North Beach, in Naden Harbour, or Masset Inlet. The key is to find sandy bottoms, preferably with eelgrass as cover for the crabs.

Detailed information is available in *Fishing the Queen Charlotte Islands* by former resident Bob Long.

Flora and Fauna

The unusual natural history of the Charlottes, combined with the area's potential for superlative outdoor recreation, is making the islands one of Canada's most desirable adventure-travel destinations. Designation of provincial, national, and international reserves for the protection of landscapes, as well as various species and their habitats, has ensured the preservation of the many special attributes of the region.

The width of the marine crossing to the islands has restricted natural influx by animals and plants. As a result the islands are populated by a slightly impoverished and more specialized assembly of species (see checklists at back of book). There is also a much higher than normal percentage of fauna and flora that are unique to the islands (i.e. not found elsewhere in Canada). There are endemic subspecies of birds, mammals, and fishes. At one time the islands supported a unique species of caribou, now unfortunately extinct. There are several full species of insects found here, and more are expected to be discovered.

Among plants, there are a dozen examples of species found only on the Charlottes. Not surprisingly in this moist climate, many are mosses. Another two dozen plants are examples of disjunct populations. This means they are separated from their expected distribution by great distances. For example, some are normally found in Japan, Asia, and Scotland. Possibly they were left on the Charlottes after finding refuge on an unglaciated part of the islands during the Ice Age which wiped out intervening plants.

These ecological oddities have given rise to the popular promotion of the islands as the "Galapagos of Canada." The Galapagos Islands of equatorial Ecuador are famous for the evolutionary distinctions of their wildlife, originally studied by Charles Darwin. Biological parallels are evident, as they are on any isolated islands. For the most part we feel the phrase does better for promotion than application, as it gives a distorted expectation of the wildlife to be expected. Nevertheless, knowledgeable birders, botanists, nature photographers, and other enthusiasts will be delighted with what they can find here. Some reading prior to arriving will do much to enhance your pleasure. *Islands at the Edge: Preserving the Queen Charlotte Islands Wilderness* is your best single introduction to the outstanding natural history of these islands today.

The Haida People

The first people to arrive on this rich offshore territory were the Haida, who have lived here as long as 10,000 years. Haida means "the people" in their language, and Haida Gwaii refers to the Charlottes, their homeland. At the height of their power the Haida were estimated to number about 6000 people. In pre-contact time their territory extended to islands south of present-day Wrangell on the Alaskan panhandle, though they no longer occupy or claim that area.

Surrounded by water, the Haida were expert mariners, adept at exploiting the bounty of the marine environment. The expanse of ocean not only offered protection from invasion, but also provided rich, easily-attainable sustenance year-round. During the warm months they spent time collecting food, travelling, and trading. During the winter they concentrated in large villages at about a dozen coastal locations around Haida Gwaii. In the warmth of their lodges, great energy was put into social and cultural activities.

The annual pattern of mainland tribes was similar, though few of them reached the wealth and power of the status-conscious Haida. Nevertheless, the neighbouring Tsimshian had food items, hides, and other natural resources not present on the islands. Thus the tribes traded frequently among themselves. The contact was not always peaceful, however. Haida ferocity in battle was renown, as they also raided mainlanders in retribution for insults, and to capture slaves and booty. Sometimes it seemed they just enjoyed a good fight. It must have been with some trepidation that mainlanders watched Haida canoes approach their villages. They could never be sure whether it would be clubs or trade canoes that the visitors would offer.

The moderate maritime climate and the year-round abundance of food provided the Haida with the leisure time to develop a complex culture. By all accounts these people were shrewd, courageous, dignified, and creative. Though much was irretrievably lost during the colonial period, the Haida are now reviving and reshaping many age-old traditions. They were, and remain, one of the most respected native nations on the Northwest Coast. Today their political action and land claims are a vanguard of aboriginal action in the province. These major issues have remained without resolution for over a century.

The revival of Haida art is one of the most appreciated aspects in this process. Many native artisans have achieved international reputations. They are weavers, and carvers of silver, gold, argillite (a soft black shale quarried on Slatechuck Mountain), and cedar wood. An item from these masters of myth makes an ideal memento of your visit. Band council offices will direct you to the homes of individual artists, or you might purchase something at one of the better gift shops.

Hunting

Possibly the first recreational hunter in the Charlottes was Charles Sheldon, who searched for Dawson caribou here in November of 1906. He persistently endured three weeks of ghastly weather in unsuccessful pursuit of that now-extinct animal. Despite his difficulties he writes with a keen interest in natural history, and his observations in *The Wilderness of the North Pacific Coast Islands* provide an interesting perspective of those times.

Modern hunters like the Charlottes for the nine month season and high limits on deer. Sitka or coastal mule deer were originally introduced to provide islanders with a fresh meat source. With no natural predators on the islands, however, they soon became over-abundant. Though small in stature, these deer are tender and flavourful. Hunting has reduced deer numbers near populated areas, but they are still plentiful on backroads. Their tolerance of approach make them particularly popular with bow hunters. Larger bucks are most cautious about showing themselves. The locals claim deer hunting to be most productive during the rut in November. When it snows the animals will forage for kelp washed on the beaches. At any time of year they can be found in grassy meadows, roadsides, and estuaries.

There is limited hunting for a small elk herd which was introduced on Graham Island. Unlike their deer cousins, these animals have not expanded their numbers, and rarely stray from territory on the upper Tlell River watershed.

Hunters interested in black bear are attracted to the Queen Charlottes by the trophy-sized animals taken here. The particular

Black bear (*Ursus americanus*) tracks with a 15 cm (6 in) ruler. The skull measurements of the Charlotte sub-species are the largest on this continent. Bears can be expected on any island, and precautions must be taken in camp.

subspecies which lives on the islands is the largest in North America. Hunters concentrate for them on beaches and tidal estuaries of Moresby Island, where bears feed on crabs and grasses. In the fall the bears concentrate along salmon streams. They are even found occasionally on small islands, but these are poor locations to hunt. The question of continued hunting within the South Moresby National Park Reserve is presently under review. All out-of-province big game hunters are required to hire a licenced guide. Two such guides live on the Charlottes.

There is some waterfowl hunting on the Charlottes as well, though not anything for which one would plan a trip exclusively. Protected bays with large estuary flats are favoured by Canada Geese and ducks. These birds concentrate when storms keep them off migration flights. No hunting or discharge of firearms is permitted in Naikoon Provincial Park from April 1st to September 1st. For more information, contact:

Ministry of Environment
Conservation Officer Service
Box 370
Queen Charlotte City, B.C. V0T 1S0
(604) 559-8431

The Metric System

In 1975 Canada began its conversion to the internationally-accepted method of measurement, the metric system. By 1984 we were all using this standard, much to the confusion of people who felt they were too old to learn new tricks, and to our American visitors. Until everyone is trained in metric use, many publications continue to use both systems for the convenience of readers. After each unit of measure in this book is the converted Imperial system equivalent in parentheses. For the uninitiated, here are the abbreviations of metric weights and measures which will appear in this book:

millimetre	mm	length
metre	m	length
kilometre	km	length
kilogram	kg	weight
hectares	ha	area
celsius	°C	temperature

Museums

One of the best introductions to life in the islands is to be found in the Queen Charlotte Islands Museum at Skidegate. A showpiece for small museums, it is built on a cliff overlooking the Islands of Skidegate Inlet. From the deck facing the inlet, you can spot migrating gray whales in spring. Inside the cedar building are displays of native art, natural history, and European settlement. The collection is attractively laid out, but you may want to buy a book to get detailed information on the artifacts and pioneers. Additional gift shops in Sandspit and Charlotte have good selections of new and antiquarian books about the region. The museum is open 9 a.m. to 5 p.m. from May to September, and from 1 p.m. to 5 p.m. the rest of the year.

In Haida is the Ed Jones Museum, a private museum in a former schoolhouse which has items from both pre- and post-European periods. Its odd assortment of artifacts is nonetheless interesting as many are not seen elsewhere on the islands and have significant regional importance. This museum is usually open each day in the summer. Port Clements's new museum focuses on logging, commercial fishing and farming equipment. Work is still progressing on this collection. Though operating in both summer and winter, hours are not fixed.

Navigation

Probably the greatest threat to the novice recreationist is the sea. For all boaters we highly recommend the use of nautical charts. Unlike topographic maps, charts mark navigational aids, current flows, and marine hazards. They measure depths in fathoms, which helps anglers find shallows for fishing. Depths are recorded during tidal lows, enabling predictable passage through shallow areas.

They are indispensable for navigation at night and in fog (when you'll also require a compass). A compact method of keeping them dry is to seal two back to back within plastic at a commercial laminators. Do-it-yourselfers use clear shelf covering, but we don't care for the liquid coatings you paint on. Rolling coated charts prevents leaks along folded seams.

Tide tables are mandatory for mariners and beachcombers alike. They are published annually by the Federal Department of Fisheries and Oceans, and list the height and time of high and low tides each day. The closest measuring station to the Charlottes is Prince Rupert on the mainland. Since tides reach there ahead of the islands, one hour must be added for Skidegate Inlet and two hours for Masset Inlet. Add another hour during Pacific Daylight Saving Time, which is effective summer and fall. Obviously a watch is necessary even in backcountry areas. Detailed information is included with the tables or can be gleaned from almost any local mariner. Also see **Climate and Clothing** section of this chapter.

Tide tables and charts are available in coastal sporting goods and marine supply stores or can be mail-ordered from:

> Canadian Hydrographic Service
> Chart Distribution & Sales
> Box 6000
> Sidney, B.C. V8L 4B2

Tide tables covering the Queen Charlottes are *Volume 6: Barkley Sound and Discovery Passage to Dixon Entrance.* Marine Charts covering all marine areas mentioned in this book are:

Dixon Entrance 3802
Masset Sound and Inlet 3805
Skidegate Inlet and Channel 3806
Juan Perez Sound 3808
Carpenter Bay to Burnaby Island 3809
Cape St. James to Houston Stewart Channel 3825
Cape St. James to Cumshewa Inlet & Tasu Sound . 3853
Port Luis to Langara Island 3868
Skidegate Channel to Tain Rock (Rennell Sound) . 3869
Selwyn Inlet to Lawn Point 3894
Plans — Dixon Entrance 3895
Atli Inlet to Selwyn Inlet 3807

Permits for Haida Reserves

When entering abandoned Haida villages and Indian reserves, permission must be obtained beforehand from the appropriate band office. You will be considered a trespasser without it. Sites on Graham and Langara islands are looked after by the band council in the village of Haida (626-3337). All other villages are administered by the Skidegate Band Council. In 1989 a charge of $25.00 per person was made by the Skidegate Band. This fee covered all of the band's former villages, including those within the national park reserve. Native watchmen are posted most summers at popular sites including Hotspring Island, and ask for evidence of payment. Visitors on organized tours will be covered by a blanket permit issued to the operator.

You should be aware that such permits are presently a very sensitive issue. Legally, the Haida cannot charge a fee for any area within the park reserve except lands over which they own clear title. These are *only* the reserves at Skedans and Tanu. The Canadian Parks Service does *not* require that visitors purchase permits to visit any public lands, including Hotspring Island, Ninstints Village or Windy Bay.

Permits may be obtained by mail or personal application. The office issuing them is:

Haida Gwaii Watchmen
Box 699
Queen Charlotte City, B.C. V0T 1S0
Telephone: (604) 559-4496

Permits for South Moresby villages are also issued by the Tourism B.C. Travel Infocentre at Joy's Island Jewellers in Charlotte. The fees are varied annually, and may vary between band offices. Overnight camping is not permitted on any Indian reserve or on Skungwai (Anthony Island).

Transportation and Travel

Also see **Chartering** above.

The government-operated car ferry *M.V. Queen of Prince Rupert* crosses Hecate Strait four times a week (less frequently in winter) from Prince Rupert on B.C.'s northern mainland. The crossing takes six to eight hours on daylight cruises, depending on marine conditions. Staterooms, dayrooms, cafeteria, bar, and a video lounge are provided. The ship docks at Skidegate Landing on Graham Island, the most populated island in the group.

In addition, two small aircraft companies provide charter and scheduled service from Prince Rupert to most places in the islands. Canadian Airlines International (CAI) flies a jet twice daily between Vancouver, B.C. and Sandspit on Moresby Island.

A mini-van meets all the CAI flights and takes passengers between the airport and Charlotte. Cars and trucks can be rented in Sandspit, Charlotte, and Masset. Taxis are available in all communities, and as well, a water taxi crosses Skidegate Inlet after ferry hours. Hitch-hikers have a good chance for a quick pick-up on most island roads.

Graham and Moresby islands are connected by a small open-deck ferry, the *M. V. Kwuna*, which runs on a frequent schedule. The *Kwuna* unites the Yellowhead Highway No. 16, a paved route on which all the communities are located. Other than the highway and a few residential roads, all roads on the islands are private.

Private all-weather gravel-surfaced backroads are owned and maintained by logging companies. Reaching some locations in this book means travelling on them. The islands are a maze of such routes. They are well-maintained and open to the public under certain conditions. Information on truck activity and maps must be obtained from the local corporate offices. On Graham Island contact MacMillan Bloedel Ltd.; on Moresby Island, Fletcher Challenge Canada. Follow their instructions carefully. These roads are used by off-highway trucks bearing loads nearly double the weight of anything you've seen before. Meeting a loaded logging truck on a sudden curve is equivalent to looking down the gunbarrel of an armoured tank. Always drive with your headlights on. Never venture onto the roads during working hours.

Fletcher Challenge Canada has a tourist information centre operating from May to mid-September which provides a four to five hour tour of their operations. It's a good introduction to their logging management and techniques in the Charlottes.

Addresses

Trans-Provincial Airlines
Box 224
Sandspit, B.C. V0T 1T0
Telephone: (604) 637-5355

North Coast Air Services
Box 610
Prince Rupert, B.C. V8J 3R5
Telephone: (604) 627-1351

Canadian Airlines International
Reservations and Information:
   Toll-free 1-800-426-7000 within U.S. or (206) 433-5088 in Seattle area. Phone numbers vary within Canada. Consult your directory yellow pages.

Fletcher Challenge Canada
Box 470
Sandspit, B.C. V0T 1T0
Telephone: (604) 637-5436
Winter number:
   (604) 637-5323

MacMillan Bloedel Ltd.
Queen Charlotte Division
Box 10
Juskatla, B.C. V0T 1J0
Telephone: (604) 557-4212
In Q.C. City: (604) 559-4224

B.C. Ferry Corporation
Reservations Centre
1112 Fort Street
Victoria, B.C. V8V 4V2
   Telephone: (604) 386-3431 or toll-free from Vancouver, B.C., 669-1211. The Reservations Centre is open daily from 7 a.m. to 10 p.m.

Warning!

   We would be most remiss if we did not warn you of one particular feature about the Queen Charlotte Islands. This is the curious effect of the waters of St. Mary's Spring. The location of the spring is marked by a chainsaw carving of a woman on the side of Yellowhead Highway just north of Lawn Hill. Legend has it that whoever drinks of the spring's cool natural champagne will someday return to the islands. And it certainly has had that effect on us. We hope you will find reason to return to Haida Gwaii.

2. Birds of the Queen Charlotte Islands

The Queen Charlotte Islands are among the richest bird islands in Canada. Millions of birds visit or nest around the Charlottes every year, although the number of species found here is actually lower than on the adjacent mainland. By 1988, 218 species had been recorded on the Charlottes, compared to 444 throughout B.C. Similarly, three hundred species breed in B.C.; only seventy of these on the Charlottes. This, of course, is not surprising as remote islands predictably have fewer species. However, the unusual and rare birds of the Charlottes are guaranteed to delight casual birdwatchers and create a mecca for compulsive bird listers.

Birdwatching on the Charlottes doesn't always require binoculars. Walking along the beaches, you'll pass beneath Bald Eagles perched on overhanging branches. Among the driftwood, Song Sparrows, Dark-eyed Juncos and even Hermit Thrushes boldly continue feeding while you approach. On the water, Common Loons and White-winged Scoters are easily identified before they dive. However, if you wish to watch Sandhill Cranes dancing, witness the flight of a Peregrine Falcon, or search for Siberian shorebirds, you'll probably need a field guide, a good pair of binoculars, or a spotting scope.

Bird enthusiasts come specifically to the Charlottes to see rare, colonial, or unusual birds. Of the 218 recorded species, over seventy percent are nonperching birds. Many of these are associated with aquatic habitats. Loons, albatross, shearwaters, shorebirds and alcids fall into this category. During migration periods some of these species number into the hundreds of thousands.

Of the four species of loons, the Common and Red-throated Loon breed on lakes on the Charlottes. The smaller, lighter Red-throated Loon can take off from short stretches of water which enables them to inhabit small lakes and ponds. Although they raise their young here, they fly to the ocean for food. An estimated four hundred pairs of Red-throated Loons nest throughout the islands, giving this area one of the highest breeding densities for this species in the world.

Birders have an even stronger desire to see a third species, the Yellow-billed Loon. Although they breed exclusively in the high Arctic, individuals remain scattered along B.C.'s coast throughout the year, especially on the Charlottes. Numerous sightings occur during the spring and summer, fewer during autumn and winter. Look for them during any season in Skidegate Inlet, off Rose Spit, or in quiet inlets.

Other groups of birds travel to the Charlottes from distant areas. After breeding throughout the southern and eastern Pacific Ocean, shearwaters and albatross make their way to northern latitudes where they have been sighted from spring through fall. Of five species of shearwaters, the Sooty Shearwater is the most numerous. At least a million or more of these birds regularly spend the summer throughout Hecate Strait. Due to upwelling currents, Rose Spit is also a favourite feeding place for Sooty and several other species of shearwaters.

While searching for shearwaters, you might spot a much larger, dark-bodied bird with a wing span of two hundred cm (80 in). Sightings of Black-footed Albatross (and the even rarer Laysan Albatross) are well documented on the Charlottes. A few have been spotted in Hecate Strait, but most occur off the west coast, particularly in spring and summer.

Of the thirty-four species of shorebirds recorded, only seven are known as breeders. Two of these have made significant extensions to their normal breeding range. Semipalmated Plovers nest each spring along North and East Beach. This is far south of their main Arctic breeding grounds, and one of only a few known B.C. breeding sites. Likewise, Least Sandpipers normally nest on the tundra, but researchers have counted 90 pairs nesting at Delkatla Wildlife Refuge at Masset. This is probably the highest breeding density in the world for this species. Sanderlings do not breed here, but many stay through the winter. Annual Christmas Bird Counts have recorded the highest winter numbers of this species anywhere in Canada. Look for them sprinting along the water's edge on sandy beaches or mud flats.

The Charlottes are particularly well-known for twelve species of nesting seabirds. Over half of all of B.C.'s total seabird population, an estimated two million pairs, breed on small wooded or sparsely-vegetated islands here. These islands have protection from most predators, direct access to the ocean, and equally important, a variety of nesting sites. Of these birds, several species have interesting breeding

An immature gull has been attracted by a spawned-out salmon.
Many bird and animal scavengers are drawn to streams each fall as
the fish congregate and die. It provides a good opportunity for
wildlife photographers.

habits. Nearly seventy-five percent of the entire world population of
Ancient Murrelets and Cassin's Auklets breed on the Charlottes. The
secretive and little-known Marbled Murrelet probably nests in trees,
although no one has yet found an actual nest here.

Unlike shy murrelets, colourful puffins prefer remote rocky
islands with grass tussocks. Near the southern tip of the Charlottes,
several thousand pairs of Tufted Puffins nest in burrows on grassy
islets. But only a single nest of the less common Horned Puffin has
been discovered on the islands, although more surely breed here.

Seabirds flourish on these islands partly because colonies remain
isolated from the mainland. Isolation has also been an important
factor in the evolution of three unique subspecies. The Northern
Saw-whet Owl, Hairy Woodpecker, and Steller's Jay all live in
forest areas. They differ from their mainland relations by having
darker colours or by markings that the others don't display. Steller's
Jay is darker and lacks a noticeable white eyebrow typical of
mainland birds. Saw-whet Owls and Hairy Woodpeckers have
darker pigmentation than off-island individuals.

As most birdwatchers know, the thrill of finding a 'life bird' (i.e.
a bird never previously sighted by that birdwatcher) is perhaps
surpassed only by discovering a 'new' species (i.e. a bird never
before recorded in that area). Since the Queen Charlottes' location
lies along the migratory path of many birds, vagrants or unusual

bird wanderers occasionally appear. A Boat-tailed Grackle identified at Cape St. James must have flown here from the Gulf Coast. The Red-faced Cormorant, Aleutian Tern, and Brambling arrived from Alaska or Siberia. A Magnificent Frigatebird, sighted off Langara Island in 1981, may have come from the Galapagos Islands on the equator.

Finding migrant and resident birds on the Charlottes is a pleasant task. If you come by ferry, plan a daytime crossing and watch for oceanic birds as soon as you reach open water. The ferry docks in Skidegate Inlet, one of the better island birding spots. Kagan Bay, Sandspit, and numerous islets host some nesting birds, as well as many migrating ducks and shorebirds.

Most seabird colonies are located in the South Moresby region. You'll require a boat or aircraft to reach them. North of Skidegate Inlet, scan the Yakoun River estuary near Port Clements. Sandhill Cranes are regulars here throughout the summer, while wintering birds include Trumpeter Swans, ducks, geese, and eagles. Delkatla Sanctuary at Masset shouldn't be missed, as its combination of water, shore, and forest habitats has attracted over 113 species. This list includes unusual vagrants such as Cattle Egrets, Marbled Godwits and Upland Sandpipers.

For us, Rose Spit remains the undisputed birding hot spot. This sandy nose hooks into Hecate Strait, attracting sea and land birds alike. Shearwaters, fulmars, auklets, and diving ducks can number into the thousands. One summer afternoon over one hundred Sooty Shearwaters crossed our spotting scope view in less than a minute. On a brisk autumn day, after waiting three hours for a pea soup fog to lift, we ticked off thirty-seven species in short order. Among them: Red Knot, Wandering Tattler, Black-legged Kittiwake, Sandhill Crane, and two Peregrine Falcons. Only a Caspian Tern, seen the day before, could have made us happier.

Seabird Islands

The seabirds that come to the Charlottes to breed each year include two species of storm-petrels, a cormorant, a gull, and eight species of alcids, or diving seabirds. They nest on smaller islands, utilizing a variety of wooded and open habitats. These range from barren rocks a few metres above high tide, to cliffs, grassy knolls, and heavily-wooded islands. Although most are difficult to survey due to their nocturnal habits and underground nests, estimated numbers range from one to two million pairs.

These birds utilize over a hundred islands. Major breeding stations, with more than 25,000 breeding pairs, exist on Langara, Hippa, Louise, Lyell, Rankine, Anthony and Kerouard islands. Seabirds have selected these sites for good reasons. In most cases the colonies are isolated from predators and free of human disturbance. Birds choose them as close as possible to their feeding areas — the pelagic waters of the eastern North Pacific. A variety of habitats exist on most islands, making it possible for several species to nest without seriously affecting one another.

Leach's and Fork-tailed Storm-Petrels are the smallest of all the seabirds on the Charlottes. Sometimes called "sea swallows", they are barely larger than those familiar insect eaters, and have a light, fluttery flight. They nest in burrows and lay a single white egg. Both sexes share incubation, which lasts about fifty days. Every few nights, in complete darkness, the colonies come alive with activity. After foraging at sea one parent returns to relieve its mate deep within the burrow. Apparently they locate each other by call. The returning adult takes over incubation while the other flies off.

Compared to the secretive storm-petrels, Pelagic Cormorants and Glaucous-winged Gulls are large and conspicuous breeding birds. Both species prefer rocky islets with little or no vegetation. The gulls occupy the flatter ground while cormorants prefer ledges and cliff faces. Flocks of gulls circling over an islet or cliffs plastered with white excrement make the colonies visible a long way off. This gives the impression that the birds are abundant, but a surprisingly low number actually breed on the Charlottes — less than five hundred pairs of cormorants and two thousand pairs of gulls.

Cormorants have the distinction of being the seabird with the greatest reproductive potential. They lay as many as six eggs and will lay a second clutch to replace damaged or stolen ones. Crows and gulls frequently grab cormorant eggs if the adults are inattentive or have been scared off the nest. It's interesting to note that cormorants, despite their vulnerability, sometimes share the same nesting islet with these same predators.

Many seabirds have solved this problem of exposed nests. These species lay their eggs in rock crevices or at the end of long burrows. The largest and most colourful burrow-nesting seabirds are Tufted Puffins and Rhinoceros Auklets. Both are dark bodied, but have

Pelagic Cormorants (*Phalacrocorax pelagicus*) in nesting colony. Two other species of cormorant resident on the Charlottes do not breed there. The species are difficult to distinguish unless seen at close range.

different bills. The puffin has a bright yellow and orange triangle similar to a parrot, hence the name "sea parrot". The Rhinoceros Auklet's thinner bill bears a small horn near the base during breeding season. Both species feed near shore, returning to their burrows on grassy slopes or in the forest floor once the sun has set. Presently, their main colonies on the Charlottes exist only in southern areas.

Ancient Murrelets and Cassin's Auklets give no visible hint as to their actual abundance. They number into the hundreds of thousands, yet are among the most secretive birds along our coast. They feed well offshore during the day, returning in total darkness to their burrows beneath the mossy forest floor. Bill snapping and twittering calls are heard as the adults crash-land beneath the trees. These vocalizations may help them orient themselves and locate their young.

Cassin's Auklets feed their single black chick regurgitated crustaceans. Forty days after hatching, the chicks fly away from the colony. Ancient Murrelet young are precocial, meaning they can feed themselves soon after birth. Within two days of hatching, two murrelet chicks leave their burrow by night. Guided by their parents' calls they scramble through the forest to the shoreline. Once on the water, they swim with their parents directly out to sea.

The Marbled Murrelet has thus far eluded attempts to locate its nest in B.C. This chocolate-coloured murrelet gathers in small groups offshore where it dives for fish. At dusk, they fly inland to destinations unknown. Evidence strongly suggests they nest in the branches of tall trees on the Charlottes. In 1953 a large hemlock was felled near Masset. Amidst the debris an adult Marbled Murrelet was found dazed but alive. Eggshell fragments were nearby but there was no evidence of a nest. This tiny bird continues to keep its secret from us.

Any discussion of seabird colonies on the Charlottes would be incomplete without mention of Peregrine Falcons and Bald Eagles, the main predators of seabirds. Between sixty and eighty pairs of Peregrine Falcons nest on the Charlottes. If nonbreeding birds are added on, the falcon population probably exceeds two hundred individuals — the highest density in Canada. Their high numbers are supported by an abundance of food, especially seabirds. They target Ancient Murrelets, Cassin's Auklets, and both species of storm-petrels. Shorebirds and smaller waterbirds are preyed on at other times of the year.

Peregrines are highly specialized predators. They pursue prey directly, catching or knocking it out of the air. During the nesting period, this activity begins at dusk, directly from the aerie. As darkness closes in, nocturnal seabirds appear from either the sea or their burrows. Peregrine Falcons wait aloft, and as the seabirds' shadowy silhouettes appear, the hunters make a swift headlong stoop. Speed, surprise, and height give deadly advantage to the predator. Falcons often make successive kills whether hungry or not, judging from the littered remains of seabirds scattered below their favourite plucking perch.

Naturally, most aeries are located close to a seabird colony. Peregrines prefer to nest on a ledge near the top of a steep cliff, utilizing overhanging roots or plants for shelter. Sometimes they'll take over an old eagle or hawk nest. Both adults share parental duties, feeding three to four young even after they become skilled fliers. This added care may be crucial to maintaining their population, as young falcons appear to have difficulty catching food on their own. This may partially account for only one young surviving through the winter.

Bald Eagles also prey on seabirds, although they lack the specialized hunting techniques demonstrated by Peregrine Falcons. Bald Eagles normally feed on fish or carrion. But on the Charlottes, at least half of their diet includes seabirds. Eagles have been observed walking through an old forest, apparently searching for stunned or disoriented murrelets. Studies have also shown that they also have a taste for gulls, shearwaters, fulmars and abalone. In winter eagles regularly eat diving ducks such as scaups and scoters.

Despite the abundance of avian predators, the populations of

Bald Eagle (*Haliaeetus leucocephalus*). These birds of prey have their greatest breeding densities in Canada on the Charlottes. Juvenile birds take about four years to attain the white head and tail feathers of maturity.

seabirds ensure that more than enough survive to maintain their high density. A far greater threat comes from a different quarter. People, fire, oil spills, logging, and introduced mammals impact seriously on seabird populations. For this reason an island in Lepas Bay, Anthony Islets, and Copper, Jeffrey, Rankine, and Kerouard islands have been designated as ecological reserves for the purpose of protecting nestling birds. Landing at any time on these islands requires a special permit.

A few simple rules, if followed, should minimize human impact at other colonies. One person walking through a colony of cormorants or gulls is enough to cause a major disruption. Gulls in particular will attack and kill chicks that cross invisible territorial boundaries. Cormorants flush from their nest when disturbed, leaving their eggs to be devoured by gulls and crows, or their young to bake in the sun. Islands that have nesting gulls and cormorants should be viewed only from the water.

Nocturnal seabird colonies seem abandoned during the day, and indeed you may be in the middle of one without knowing it. Nightfall brings thousands of adults crashing through trees and undergrowth.

This seemingly chaotic arrival is followed by a mad dash for the burrow. Domestic cats and dogs can create havoc by catching and killing adults before they locate their mates. Beach fires disorient flying birds, and if left burning, could advance into the forest. Needless to say, logging a seabird colony or a large oil spill could effectively wipe out an entire population. On any wilderness island, leave all pets on the boat (or at home), walk through the island before dark, and make sure that any fires are made below the high tide line. We have a responsibility to make sure that millions of seabirds continue to be an integral part of the Queen Charlotte Islands.

Silhouettes of Peregrin Falcon (*Falco peregrinus*) seen from below and from side. Males are smaller than females. She will be up to 54 cm (21.6 in) long, with a wingspan to 112.5 cm (45 in).

3. Marine Mammals and Reptiles

The cool, food-rich waters that surround the Queen Charlottes form part of the most favoured habitat in the Pacific for marine mammals. The Alaska current sweeps by the Charlottes' west coast, mixing tidal currents, river run-off and areas of upwelling into a high-energy, nutrient solution. Plankton, fish, and marine invertebrates thrive in this environment. In all, twenty-three species of marine mammals and a single reptile have been attracted to the area.

Marine mammals are usually large and spend most of their life in the ocean. On the Charlottes they include whales, dolphins, seals, sea lions, and the sea otter. Of the twenty-three recorded species, nine stay well offshore, ten are occasionally spotted near islands and coastlines, while six either breed or spend a significant portion of their time in nearshore waters.

Of the cetaceans (whales, porpoises, and dolphins) the gray whale is the most common and predictable on the Charlottes. These large, unassuming mammals pass through inshore waters biannually, travelling between their Arctic summering areas and Baja breeding lagoons. This 20,000 km (12,600 mi) journey is the longest undertaken by any mammal. Alone or in small groups, they travel day and night, seldom even stopping to eat. Energy is supplied by fat reserves accumulated before the journey begins.

Gray whales lack teeth, and obtain food by sucking mud from the seabed. A baleen filter in the mouth separates tiny crustaceans from mud and water. Consequently, the whales prefer shallow, fine-sediment bottoms for feeding. They migrate past the Charlottes in April and May. Watch for their smooth gray backs with a tiny dorsal fin in Skidegate Inlet, along the coast between Skidegate and Tlell, or off Rose Spit. Throughout the summer an estimated ninety to one hundred whales linger along the north coast of Graham Island.

A second group of cetaceans are distinguished by conical teeth capable of seizing fish, squid, birds, seals and sea lions. Such prey are swallowed whole or in chunks as these animals can rip, but not chew flesh. Eleven cetaceans occur here, but only three can be

45

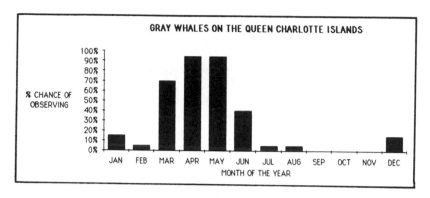

expected near shore.

The smallest of these are blunt-nosed harbour porpoises. These shy mammals prefer sheltered shorelines and waterways such as Skidegate and Cumshewa inlets. True to their disposition, they usually travel alone or in groups of two or three. Most people glimpse only a small fin disappearing beneath the surface, as these mammals vanish when approached or disturbed. Dall's porpoises are the exact opposite. These sleek, thick-bodied creatures are full of spirited curiosity. They have a reputation as the fastest marine mammal. Their bold black and white forms zip through the water, sometimes creating sudden rooster tails of spray. To the delight of boaters they love to ride bow waves. They choose fast-moving craft, but will soon vanish if you slow for a better look.

The excitement created by Dall's porpoises ranks second only to that generated by the appearance of *Orcinus orca*, the killer whale. Sighting their tall dorsal fins slicing the surface is simultaneously frightening and intriguing. But the personality and habits of these graceful marine hunters belies their reputation as undiscriminating monsters. Dr. Michael Bigg, one of the authors of *Killer Whales*, has helped rectify such myths. For years it was believed the orca ate anything that moved, and humans were thought to be fair game. Thousands of hours of observing these whales, including time in the water, have been logged. There is no valid account of aggressive behaviour toward humans in B.C. There is but a single record of a *provoked* attack on a boat. So far, Bigg has recognized three pods (family groups) of killer whales around the Charlottes. Interestingly, these particular pods appear to eat only other marine mammals.

If you travel with a pod of killer whales, you may witness an attack on a harbour seal or Steller sea lion. These pinnipeds, or fin-footed mammals, are common residents throughout the islands. They have hairy coats and 'haul out' on beaches or rocky islets. They're tolerant, sometimes allowing close approach by people and will linger after retreating into the water.

Sea lions often congregate on isolated islets where you might witness their spectacular behaviour. Often exceeding one tonne, these brown beasts seem awkward on land, but are truly graceful when plunging headlong into foaming surf. Kayakers have paddled over their massive forms, but it is wise to keep a comfortable distance as they could easily upset a small craft. At any time, but particularly during the winter months, they haul out at Rose Spit, Skedans Rocks, and Reef Island. Sea lions also congregate throughout the year at southerly Cape St. James. In the summer over eleven hundred lions return to this remote point to breed, making it the largest rookery on the Pacific Coast.

Males begin arriving on these wave-washed rocks in May and immediately establish and defend a territory. Females and immature animals arrive a few weeks later. Pregnant females give birth to a single pup soon after arriving. Within the next two weeks, while they nurse their newborn and perhaps even a yearling, they mate with one of the territorial males. The females then settle into a routine of feeding nightly at sea and returning to nurse their offspring by day. By late August this social fabric breaks apart, as most males scatter along B.C.'s coast in smaller groups. Females and pups join them later.

Sea lions anger many commercial fishermen, who accuse them falsely of depleting salmon stocks and of destroying fishing gear (which they sometimes do). Pressure is constantly applied on fisheries officials to shoot them, and at one time this was done. However, studies prove sea lions are opportunistic feeders, dining on whatever fish are most plentiful. They do not particularly favour salmon.

Harbour seals are likewise accused of gorging on salmon. Their habit of raiding spawning streams has given them a bad reputation. Despite this, they too are opportunists, catching whatever takes the least amount of energy. This fits their lifestyle well. They spend a lot of time hauled out, grooming and resting with others of their kind. But they can be spontaneous and energetic. Once we were bewildered by a splash and fleeting shape in a kelp bed. Suddenly a round head appeared and curious eyes examined us. After deciding we were harmless, a young seal playfully chomped a large kelp

47

frond, then dove after an imaginary companion.

Harbour seals seem to spend equal amounts of time on land and in water. On shore they rest, mate, give birth, and moult. You will see harbour seals hauled out on many sheltered rocks or islets throughout the Charlottes. Look for them specifically off Rose Spit, or within Masset, Skidegate, and Cumshewa inlets. Throughout South Moresby, watch for their mottled forms along the Tar Islands, at Marco Island, and in other protected areas.

Sea otters once were as plentiful as harbour seals. Smallest of all marine mammals, they were valued for their fur. British, American, and Russian traders were ruthless in their quest for these dark pelts, which fetched a fabulous price in China. So intense was their desire for wealth that greedy sailors literally traded the shirts off their backs. The Haida were willing accomplices as they vigorously traded the skins for the wonderful goods the purchasers offered. Only remnant populations of otters in Alaska and California survived the slaughter. In the past two decades, there have been two substantiated sightings in the Charlottes. Any otter you see is most likely a river otter, which are numerous throughout the Charlottes and are frequently seen in salt water.

Despite their near annihilation, sea otter populations have increased dramatically in California and Alaska. In 1911, when they were first protected by law, their numbers were so low almost no hope was given for survival. Today, studies indicate a total population of well over thirty thousand. The west coast of Vancouver Island received an introduced population in 1969 and 1970, which is slowly multiplying. The west coast of the Queen Charlottes is an excellent location for another release in B.C.

Although certainly not a mammal, it's interesting to note the largest turtle in the world has been seen (and captured by fishermen) off the Charlottes. The leatherback holds the only record for a reptile found on the Charlottes. Only a few sightings have occurred as these marine turtles tend to stay in warmer waters far to the south. Documented sightings come from Masset, Skidegate Inlet, and the South Moresby region.

The Charlottes can't claim any of these marine creatures entirely as their own, but the islands have gained a reputation as a good place to see them. Attitudes towards these marine animals have changed. Whereas we once killed them on sight, watching wildlife is now a major recreational activity. As more people experience them in their natural habitat, we recognize a kinship with them, albeit a poorly understood one. Their intelligence, care of offspring, and playfulness are qualities we share. Hopefully our experiences will blend with respect to further understand these remarkable creatures.

4. Land Mammals and Amphibians

During the last Ice Age the Queen Charlotte Islands were covered by immense sheets of ice. However thick this ice may have been, many scientists believe there were parts of the archipelago that remained ice-free. Incredibly, these pockets or refugia may have been large enough for some mammals to survive. Other species arrived on the islands afterwards, but a total of only thirteen species were present on the Charlottes when the first Europeans arrived. Unfortunately, the intruders' infested ships brought rats and mice previously unknown along the B.C. coast. The accidental importation of these four-legged foreigners marked the beginning of a rash of introductions. Today alien species on the Charlottes outnumber native mammals almost two to one.

The presence of refugia along with the natural barrier of Hecate Strait have limited widespread mammal dispersal to the Charlottes. Animals which remain isolated for a long period of time begin to differ from their relatives which have larger breeding populations. These differences may include size and colour variations, and use of different habitats. Most native mammals on the Charlottes exhibit these characteristics. For example, black bear here are the largest in North America. The marten is one of the largest on the continent and is lighter, with an orange tinge to its underfur. Even smaller mammals such as the dusky shrew, deer mouse, and ermine differ significantly. All of these are subspecies unique to the Charlottes. In contrast, the river otter and a second subspecies, the dusky shrew, resemble mainland counterparts. The otter is able to swim across the expanse of Hecate Strait, so is not genetically isolated. The shrew may have arrived relatively recently in a Haida canoe or hidden in a floating log. These exceptions provide intrigue and speculation for genetic researchers.

The Dawson caribou was the only distinct *species* of mammal on the Charlottes. Unfortunately little is known about it because the last one-seen was shot in 1908. It fitted the pattern of mammals on isolated islands, being smaller than mainland caribou. It appears to

50

A frog figure peeks from a pole at Ninstints Village. As only toads are native to these islands, did the Haida borrow this figure from mainland tribes or did early anthropologists not distinguish between the amphibians?

have maintained a tenuous existence in the bogs on Graham Island. Possibly competition from introduced deer, as well as hunting, contributed to its demise. Accounts of searching for the last of these animals are documented in Charles Sheldon's book *The Wilderness of the North Pacific Coast Islands*.

Western toads are the only native amphibian on the islands, although the Pacific treefrog has recently been introduced. Both are widely distributed in field and forest. Since toads probably did not swim across Hecate Strait, people may have brought them over, or they may have survived in glacial refugia.

The biological balance on the islands has been altered drastically by introduced animals. Undoubtedly the first rats and house mice arrived on sailing vessels as captains had no way of ridding their ships of these vermin. This was not the case with other alien introductions. By 1901 several deliberate attempts to populate the islands with deer had failed, but two subsequent introductions proved successful. Red deer from New Zealand were also released, but did not survive. Soon squirrels, beaver, elk, and raccoons were roaming the islands.

Some of the consequences of these introductions have been severe. The absence of predators and abundant food have caused a population explosion among Sitka deer. Competition among them has resulted in a change of diet — to cedar *a la bush*. Much to the chagrin of foresters, these small deer eat cedar seedlings as fast as

While mature needles are stiff and sharp, soft new tips of Sitka spruce (*Picea sitchensis*) are favoured by coastal deer. The browse lines on these saplings show their stunted growth before growing above the animals' reach.

they are planted. Researchers have partially protected plantings by placing transparent cones over the seedlings, but this adds substantial cost to tree farming.

Two other non-native mammals have also become nuisances. Raccoons have a reputation for devouring the eggs of ground-nesting birds. Since these aggressive animals are able swimmers, isolated nesting islets are well within their reach. Seabird colonies have no defense against such marauders and could be decimated due to this animal's omnivorous appetite. The beaver's habit of continually building dams has other professionals upset. Throughout the lowlands on Graham Island are countless lakes and ponds. Many were completely isolated and contained their own subspecies of stickleback. These minnow-sized fish are of great interest due to their genetic differences. Much to the chagrin of researchers, however, beaver dams have raised water levels, linking the fresh water oases, and allowing the sticklebacks to interbreed. This may seem trivial, but to biologists these fish are important. Sticklebacks have developed characteristics which ensure their survival in each lake's different environment. Beavers are destroying a rare opportunity for evolutionary study.

No amount of collective thought can predict the behaviour of an animal introduced to a new environment. Thus there is a great danger in the escape of pets and livestock. Domestic goats have already gone wild on Ramsay Island, and could have a serious impact on the vegetation if their population expands. We have heard rumours of people releasing snakes, ferrets, and mink. Visitors must keep their pets leashed, particularly in wild areas. Given the knowledge of what has happened, and the uncertainty of what could happen, it would be an act of selfishness and indifference to make any further introductions to the Queen Charlottes.

5. Crossing Hecate Strait

Getting There

Many people cross Hecate Strait by boat. The B.C. ferry *Queen of Prince Rupert* has scheduled crossings between Prince Rupert on the mainland coast and Skidegate Landing on the Queen Charlottes. This ship can accommodate recreational vehicles of all types, cars, bicycles, and walk-on passengers. You can even carry on your kayaks! The upper decks have several lounges, a restaurant, and overnight berths. One lounge becomes an informal sleeping area after 10:00 p.m. Scheduled flights via two small airlines also cross Hecate Strait from Prince Rupert to Sandspit, Queen Charlotte City, and Masset.

The ferry ride across Hecate Strait is one of the longest and most interesting ferry rides across open water in Canada. Upon arriving at Prince Rupert, put your problems in your pocket, but leave space for thrills and adventure. A six- to eight-hour ocean cruise to the famous Misty Isles lies ahead! Once aboard, claim a couch near the large windows, keep binoculars ready, and settle in for the crossing. In summer Hecate is usually calm. But even when swells grow, the clouds move in and spray sweeps the decks, the rougher side of Hecate's personality can still be appreciated.

For the first hour you travel through the busy waters of Chatham Sound. This sheltered waterway is part of the Inside Passage, a marine route which virtually avoids the open sea between Alaska and Vancouver Island. Watch for other passenger ships, freighters, tugs, yachts, fishboats, and pleasure craft travelling in all directions. The Hecate trip really begins as the ferry passes through Edye Pass. You might expect this broad expanse of water to be deep. In fact, for most of its 200 km (126 mi) length, Hecate Strait averages only seventeen fathoms in depth (31 m or 102 ft). At the northern end, the bottom comes to within a mere seven fathoms (13 metres or 43 ft) of the surface. The strait links shallow Dixon Entrance in the north with Queen Charlotte Sound in the south.

The explanation for the shallowness of the basin is buried in geologic time. Several times in the last million years, sheets of ice covered both the Queen Charlotte Islands and the mainland. The ice, carrying large quantities of rock and sediment, moved slowly from the mountains to the sea. Here it either floated away as icebergs or melted. The debris that was carried with the ice was deposited in ever-increasing amounts in Hecate Strait. Exploratory offshore drilling by oil companies has revealed sediment in the sea bed over three kilometres (1.8 mi) deep.

Such shallows can produce quick change. The strait acts to magnify tidal flows, and when combined with strong winds, extremely large waves can result. Hecate Strait can erupt into a frenzy within hours, and has a reputation as one of the roughest stretches of water on the Pacific Ocean. This is particularly true during seasonal gales, when ferry departures sometimes have to be postponed for as much as forty-eight hours. As Second Officer David Parry summed up these rough rides, "If you want a real pounding, you need to cross in the winter."

Boats have long linked the Charlottes with the 'outside'. The Haida regularly paddled huge canoes across Hecate Strait on raiding and trading forays. In his book *In the Wake of the War Canoe*, Reverend William Collison, first missionary on the Charlottes, recounts crossing Hecate for the first time:

> As the wind increased the sea arose and threatened to engulf our frail bark in its yawning depths. In six hours we had lost all sight of land, and even the mountain tops had disappeared. None of us were able to retain our seats on the thwarts, nor would it have been well to have done so, as they are only sewn to the sides of the canoe with thongs of cedar withes, and might easily have given way under the increased strain. In addition she rode better with the ballast low down, consequently all save the steersman had to remain huddled up in the bottom of the canoe. An occasional wave broke over us, which kept us all on the alert, and soon all four of our young sailors were seized with that dread ailment *mal de mer*. I, together with my steersman and bowman, remained unaffected for which I felt thankful, as it required all our efforts to keep our frail craft afloat. ". . . Just as we were congratulating ourselves on our success we sighted a

55

This engraving by western artist Frederick Remington first appeared in 1891. Though not of a Haida canoe, the paddling scene is authentic. The steersman holds his paddle to slice the oncoming wave to reduce its impact.

dark ridge or wall of water rushing up rapidly towards us from the south. Apprehensive of being swamped or capsized, we furled sail, and, grasping our paddles, headed our canoe around to meet the approaching danger. It proved to be but the turn of the incoming tide, which rushes shoreward from the ocean at this point with great force.

After thirteen hours at sea the tired crew staggered ashore on Rose Spit to cook their first food.

The waters of Hecate Strait are as rich in fish as they are in history. At one time Prince Rupert was known as the halibut capital of the world, but over-fishing has severely reduced this region's catch. Nevertheless commercial fishermen still lay out mile-long strings for halibut and smaller ground-fish. In May or June you may notice numbered scotchmen, or buoys, which mark the ends of their sets. These long-lines lie on the bottom with baited hooks at intervals while the boat lays other strings. Hecate Strait is also fished heavily by trollers looking for salmon. These smaller boats drag lures from lines hung out on poles and catch fish individually. Other methods are also used.

A large number and variety of seabirds spend the summer in the strait. Shearwaters are recognized by their habit of skimming low over the waves. Their sabre-like wings sometimes appear to shear the swells, hence their name. These birds return south before winter storms begin.

Shearwaters are usually seen in open water. Stay close to a window, or better still, stand outside on the forward deck. Of four species recorded in Hecate Strait, Sooty Shearwaters are the most numerous. Watch for their dark bodies gliding effortlessly over the waves or sitting duck-like in groups of fifteen to twenty. Sometimes they mass in flocks of over a hundred thousand and sightings of a quarter million have been documented here.

Shearwaters prefer seas where squid and small oceanic fish are plentiful. This special diet is also preferred by two other types of oceanic birds — the gull-like fulmar and the larger Black-footed Albatross. Both these species are uncommon here, making it all the more thrilling to spot one. Bird enthusiasts sometimes go to a lot of expense chartering vessels to see such species. But since some pelagic birds spend up to five months in Hecate Strait, the ferry is your chance for some inexpensive birding.

Birdwatchers will notice the bird fauna change as the Charlottes appear. The numbers of shearwaters taper off, replaced by grebes, Pigeon Guillemots, and scoters. Approaching Lawn Hill along the coastline of Graham Island, the ferry makes a sharp turn. It follows an ocean trench visible only by depth sounder. Too soon, you'll pass the native community of Skidegate, Torrens and Jewel islands, and ease into the dock at Skidegate Landing. You've entered Skidegate Inlet, one of the most interesting inlets on the Charlottes, and worthy of its own chapter.

Skidegate Inlet to Gray Bay

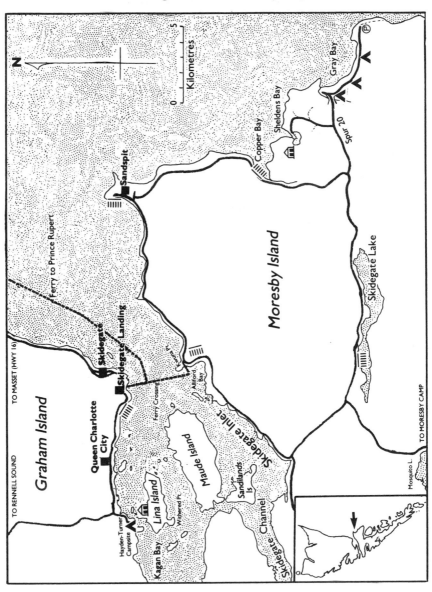

6. Around Skidegate Inlet

Getting There

For many visitors the first close-up view of the Queen Charlotte Islands is of Skidegate Inlet. This marine channel separates Graham and Moresby, the largest islands in the chain. The motor vessel *Queen of Prince Rupert* off-loads vehicles and passengers in a cove on Graham Island within this inlet. Aircraft and helicopters arrive at a nearby concrete ramp, as well as at Sandspit airport on Moresby. Small boats enter Skidegate Inlet from Hecate Strait or from the west via narrow Skidegate Channel.

To reach Hayden-Turner Campsite, drive through Queen Charlotte City 1.8 km (1.1 mi) past the Elementary-Secondary School. At this municipal park, six large campsites have tables, firepits, and nearby pit toilets. Fresh water is available in Charlotte. The nearest RV park with full hookups is in Sandspit.

Graham Island on the north and Moresby Island on the south face one other across Skidegate Inlet. Over 12 km (7.5 mi) wide at its eastern mouth, Skidegate Inlet squeezes between islands and mountains for 30 km (19 mi) before becoming Skidegate Channel, which connects to the west coast. These waterways provide terrific opportunities to explore homesteads and old Haida village sites, watch seabirds or marine mammals, find fossils and intertidal life, and fish for salmon. Skidegate Inlet lends itself nicely for exploration by either boat or car, so this chapter has two sections.

Exploration By Boat

You can begin a circle trip around the inlet at the cement airplane ramp located between Skidegate Landing and Queen Charlotte City. Boats can be launched here even at low tide, there is plenty of parking, and a phone booth is available. Unfortunately, strong westerly winds make launching troublesome at times. Under adverse conditions you may opt to take the shuttle ferry *M.V.Kwuna* across to Moresby Island. Other ramps can be used at Skidegate Landing and Alliford Bay (the ferry landings) or the

This ammonite (*Dubariceras freboldi*) from Maude
Island is an important fossil in Jurassic paleontology of
North America. Related to the modern nautilus, this
marine mollusc lived here about 195 million years ago.

government dock in Sandspit. Small boats may navigate safely throughout the inlet, but a chart is essential as numerous rocks make boating hazardous for the unprepared.

Before jumping aboard at the airplane ramp, examine some of the boulders along the beach. Ammonites (extinct coiled marine shells) and clams almost pop from the rocks, their black fossils contrasting sharply with the sandstone which imprisons them. Many fossil sites have been discovered in Skidegate Inlet, imprints of marine life 140 million years ago.

Once underway, head toward Queen Charlotte City. You'll pass exquisite sand beaches on Maple, Gooden, and Roderick islands. Modern homesteads have been built on some of these islands — please respect private property.

One of the largest islands, Lina, has evidence of many previous inhabitants. Haida formerly dwelt in at least three places around Lina's perimeter. On the extreme east end, several tiny islets shelter a clearing which was the site of Lina Village. Only depressions in the tall grass give any hint of the former houses.

During pioneering days, eight white families homesteaded elsewhere on the island. Their buildings have vanished as well, a scenario typical of the Charlottes. Farmers have come and gone, but their gardens remain. By searching carefully along the south shore you should find gnarled apple trees, an over-sized holly tree, and several flowering shrubs. Tall stems of foxglove, an introduced flower, often mark these former cultivations throughout the islands.

A more diligent search is required to find the petroglyphs on Lina Island. Four faint designs discovered in 1972 may be found at the high tide line near Withered Point. Two carvings resemble faces, the others consist of mysterious circular motifs.

After rounding Withered Point, you'll find yourself in Kagan Bay. Also known as Waterfowl Bay, this shallow basin lives up to its name. In mid-summer we recorded ten bird species jammed together on one small rock. Thousands of scoters and grebes pause here during their migrations. Numerous rocks, islets, and extensive mud flats guarantee several hours of good birdwatching. Kagan Bay and connecting Maude Channel are also pleasant places to canoe or kayak. Tidal currents swirl past the tips of some islands, creating eddies and small whirlpools.

Depending on the amount of time available, you have two options while in Maude Channel. You might try the short-cut between Maude and Graham Island. This leads west via Skidegate Channel. Kayakers in particular will enjoy the East and West Narrows, since the 4 m (12 ft) tidal difference turns the narrows into a swift river. To reach the open Pacific you'll have to paddle over 30 km (18.9 mi). If you turn east past Sandilands Island, explore the south side of Maude Island.

This sausage-shaped island bears scars of successive logging operations. Fortunately lush spruce and hemlock growth covers the wounds. Boats can usually motor right next to the sheer cliffs along this side. At low tide you'll be treated to a spectacular array of intertidal life. Thousands of brown or white anemones dangle from the cliff face like dripping wax. Water normally supports their characteristic barrel shape, but their muscles stretch as the tide drops. Fossils discovered along this shoreline have made Maude Island famous within the geologic community. Each layer of rock has such fine specimens that they have become a comparative base for others of this time period throughout the world.

At the extreme east end of Maude Island look for the grass-covered point and a tiny island. Haina Village or Sunshine-Town was located here, but has the sad distinction of being a transition village. As the west coast villages were decimated by disease in the late 1800s, survivors moved to this village site. Haida homes and totems were raised alongside a Methodist church. By 1893 the residents moved again to form the larger community of Skidegate Mission. As this is an Indian reserve, you need permission to explore it.

Pigeon Guillemots (*Cepphus columba*) in summer plumage.
These Charlotte residents nest in crevices on sea cliffs. They are
related to puffins and auklets.

With Maude Island behind you, head for the islets near Kwuna
Point. Three seabird species nest on these tiny islets. Watch for
Pigeon Guillemots with black bodies and white wing patches. As
they scoot across the water or squat on a favourite rock, their
brilliant red legs leave no doubt as to their identity. Often gathering
near kelp beds, they dive in search of skinny, eel-like fish called
blennies. They can hold several in their bills as they return to nests
under logs or in rock crevices.

Glaucous-winged Gulls also feed and nest here. Unlike
guillemots, they build exposed nests on islets with little or no
vegetation. In June and early July the islets appear snowy as parents
incubate their speckled eggs. Once hatched, the scruffy grey chicks
scamper from the nest. By summer's end they're large enough to
fend for themselves.

The third nesting seabird may be harder to find. Almost the size
of gulls, Black Oystercatchers are the buffoons of the inlet. Like a
clown with an exaggerated appendage, this absurd, red-billed
shorebird balances its chunky body on elongated pink legs. A
golden eye rimmed in red completes the costume. With such brilliant
coloration the Oystercatcher might seem an easy bird to spot,
however they prefer secluded islets where they lay their eggs just
above the high tide line. Look for adults resting on boulders or
flying together offshore. Their loud, monotonous "queep" carries
halfway across the inlet.

In September anglers easily outnumber birds around these islets.

American Black Oystercatchers (*Haematopus bachmanii*) are unmistakable with their robust red bill and pink feet. While they do eat small molluscs, they can't catch oysters since those shellfish live below the tide line.

They are attracted by coho salmon which seem to like the deep clear waters around Maude Island and nearby Kwuna Point. For many years the popular local technique was drift fishing with Buzz Bombs or similar lures. Fishermen now take a creative approach, spin-casting these lures and different shiny spoons over ledges and near submerged rocks. Trollers prefer flashers and hoochies, with colours being their best-kept secret. We trolled a flasher with a 'broken back' and a green hoochie for 30 minute intervals. During line checks a few more ounces of weight were added if nothing touched the lure. These fish feed primarily near the surface.

Another popular fishing method involves criss-crossing the shoals near Sandspit. Although these shallow waters are exposed to the seas of Hecate Strait, local anglers love to spend long summer evenings out here fantasizing of bent rods and whirring reels. During June and July coho about 2 kg (5 lb) feed in water up to 30 m (100 ft) deep. We enjoyed being out in the open, but only a small pink salmon took our hoochie. Unfortunately our timing was off. We would have done better had we fished here in the fall. Skidegate's fishing really gets going in late September and remains productive throughout October. Nice catches at that time of the year reach 7 kg (16 lb), but winners in the annual coho derby usually weigh in 9 kg (20 lb) beauties.

Whether your pleasure be fishing, boating, birding, or exploring, eventually you'll have to head in. Leave Alliford Bay, pass Maude Island, and cross Bearskin Bay. A visit to Torrens and Jewel islands makes a delightful detour during nice weather. A pebble beach on Torrens Island makes landing easy, and you might enjoy a picnic amid the driftwood or search for deer in the undergrowth. Make your way back to the boat ramp by following the shoreline back into Skidegate Inlet.

Exploration By Car

Begin your road trip around Skidegate Inlet from the B.C. Ferry dock at Skidegate Landing. The shuttle ferry *M. V. Kwuna* transports vehicles and passengers from here to Alliford Bay across the inlet. The twenty-minute ride is a must if you don't have an opportunity to tour the inlet in your own craft. A small lounge provides protected viewing during rain, but on nice days outside on deck is the place to be. We've seen storm-petrels in spring, porpoises in the summer, and hundreds of migrating birds in the fall. And keep a sharp lookout for whales.

Gray whales pass by here twice each year. They travel through once in spring and again in very late fall, to and from the Arctic Ocean. Their feeding habits explain why they linger around shallow areas within this inlet. Grays position their jaws sideways, very close to a sandy bottom. By folding their lips outwards and quickly retracting their tongue, they suck in large amounts of sand and living organisms. A baleen plate filters unwanted sand and water, retaining thousands of tiny, 2 or 3 cm (1 in) long amphipods. Between each feed, they usually surface to breathe. Watch for a 2 m (6 ft) lollipop-shaped spout, or a smooth, mottled gray back with a small dorsal fin.

Alliford Bay is tucked behind several tiny islets and a small peninsula. Disembark from the ferry and walk to nearby Oliver or Fossil Point. You reach this small point after passing through a log-sorting area and following a gravel road next to the beach. On a falling tide, follow the shoreline out to the point. Below the high tide line virtually every rock has fossil clams, snails, or pen-shaped belemnites. Research by the Geological Survey of Canada has revealed that these creatures lived between 65 and 141 million years ago during eras called the Jurassic and Cretaceous Periods. Such fossils are valuable to scientists attempting to reconstruct life and land processes of those times.

From Alliford Bay, Beach Road follows the shore to Sandspit airport. Homes and small businesses parallel this 14.6 km (9.1 mi)

Balancing rock is an erratic, dropped long ago by glaciers, and has a different composition than the bedrock it rests on. To find it, follow the trail from the leaping deer sign on the highway just north of Skidegate.

paved route. Heading south from Sandspit, Copper Bay Road will take you to Gray Bay, Skidegate Lake, Pallant Creek, and Cumshewa Inlet. Well-maintained logging roads allow you to travel a circle beginning and ending at the Alliford Bay ferry. Many people drive this loop for a day's outing. See **Gray Bay** or **Pallant Creek Fish Hatchery** chapters for more information.

An alternative to driving the backroads is the spit itself. It can be reached by a trail through beach grass from the government dock at the airport. The shallow water covering the spit attracts all types of migrating shorebirds. Further out, thousands of scoters may cover the water like a dark sheet. Their spring arrival coincides with that of spawning Pacific herring. If a mischievous eagle or an over-zealous boater puts them to flight, their wings produce a high pitched tremulous whistling.

Anglers like the spit as much as do birdwatchers. On incoming tides, winds and currents can combine to form large eddies within casting distance of shore. Buzz Bombs or Crocodiles cast into the swirling water have hooked many coho salmon.

Don't forget your ferry return to Graham Island. Sailing times are posted at both docks. On several occasions we've missed the boat due to long vehicle lineups. Arrive at least half an hour before departure to ensure a space on board. The extra time will be well spent beachcombing nearby.

7. Rennell Sound

Getting There

Rennell Sound on the west coast can be reached easily by road or boat. Gravel roads leading to the sound begin at Queen Charlotte City and Juskatla. From the MacMillan Bloedel truck repair shop in Charlotte the route leads north for 22 km (13.8 mi) to the Rennell junction. An alternate route leads from Juskatla southward through the interior for about 45 km (28.3 mi) until meeting the same turn-off to Rennell. Toward the coast the terrain steepens, and after 12 km (7.5 mi) of turns and switchbacks, the sound comes into view.

A steep hill with an eighteen to twenty percent grade separates this viewpoint from the ocean below. The grade may appear unpassable, but all types of recreational vehicles have made it down and back up. If you have a heavy trailer, you can drop it temporarily at the top. Check the 1 km (0.6 mi) grade before towing a load down.

Every weekday logging trucks travel these roads from 7:00 a.m. to 5:30 p.m. During these hours, you must report to the MacMillan Bloedel office to obtain a road map and current information.

> MacMillan Bloedel Limited:
> Juskatla office: (604) 557-4212
> Charlotte shop: (604) 559-4224

Within an hour of driving from Charlotte, you'll reach a modest viewpoint overlooking Rennell Sound. On a bright day the aquamarine swells below shimmer with the promise of many discoveries. The sound measures 15 km (9.4 mi) across its mouth and bites 30 km (18.9 mi) into Graham Island. It has a wonderful variety of beaches, hidden coves, wildlife and camping sites, as well as excellent fishing and boating. These make an ideal combination for experiencing the power, beauty, and excitement of the open ocean.

After reaching the base of the steep hill, a T intersection yields two options. A right turn offers the most variety, especially for those who don't have a boat. Within one minute, you will pass a B.C. Forest Service recreation site. Further along the rough road

Rennell Sound

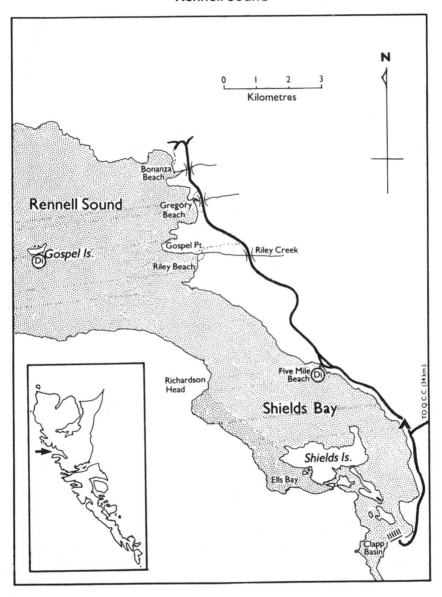

Rennell Sound

Bonanza Beach

Gregory Beach

Gospel Is.

Gospel Pt.

Riley Creek

Riley Beach

Richardson Head

Five Mile Beach

Shields Bay

Shields Is.

Ells Bay

Clapp Basin

TO Q.C.C. (34 km.)

0 1 2 3
Kilometres

N

leads to hiking trails, walk-in campsites, and sandy beaches. A left turn at the intersection takes you 4 km (2.5 mi) to a rough boat ramp and several rustic camping areas. We recommend starting your exploration at the recreation site.

Here the B.C. Forest Service has cleared seven spaces large enough for tents or trailers. Tables and pit toilets have been built, and a clear creek flows by the camp. No fees are collected. A sign outlines public roads, four beach trails, and a scuba diving area. Allow at least a day to explore these west coast beaches.

The first trail begins near the dry land log sorting area, which can't be missed as you continue 3 km (1.8 mi) past the campsite. The road splits here. Take the left fork through the sorting area and watch for a sign for Five Mile Beach. It's a two minute walk down to the water's edge. At low tide, an isthmus connects with a tiny island. Sharp rocks splashed by Pacific swells support a good sampling of intertidal life. Look for abalone and turban snails on the rocks. If you're lucky, *Dentalium* — the 'money tusk' shell might be discovered on the beach. These thin white tubes were a form of native currency, their value being determined by length. Shells over 7 cm (3 in) were so valuable that only Haida chiefs owned them.

Six kilometres (3.7 mi) further you'll pass the Riley Creek trailhead, decorated with fluorescent markers. A pleasant forty-five minute walk along this moist trail introduces you to an ancient west coast forest. Large hemlock, cedar and spruce shield a moss-draped forest floor from sunlight. Penetrating rays highlight pale flowers and sparkling pools within Riley Creek. A log bridge crosses the creek and leads to the largest portion of the beach, ten minutes farther along. Leave room in your packsack for beachcombing treasures, and schedule time to explore the headlands.

These outings may whet your appetite for the longer Gregory and Bonanza Beaches. To reach them, drive past the Riley pull-out for 3 - 5 km (1.8 - 3.1 mi). Orange fluorescent markers on brown posts indicate vehicle pull-outs and trailheads. Short trails easily managed even by small children lead directly to sand and surf. Like Riley Beach, each has a few tent sites, drinking water, and unobstructed views of the open sea.

Bedrock at both ends of these beaches contains the soft sand. Heavy surf often breaks against these outcrops with tremendous force. Only creatures that can withstand the impact of tonnes of water survive such exposure. Chalk-coloured gooseneck barnacles and large California mussels are permanent residents of this violent world. The barnacles cement themselves with a tough leathery neck. California mussels use fibrous strands as anchors on hard surfaces. Sea stars such as Pisaster move slowly over beds of mussels and barnacles. Their hundreds of tube feet serve to hold the animal firmly when waves smash over them. They also assist feeding. The tube feet pry mussel shells apart, then the starfish inserts its stomach and digests the shell's contents. What a way to go!

Exposed headlands abound with intertidal life at low tide. But as the tide turns and the channels fill, our attention shifts to wave-watching. Rising water forces a retreat to higher ground as waves race up the channels to explode into seething froth. The titanic force is powerful, yet spell-binding.

These Pacific swells often deposit unusual articles such as tropical plants, bits of sea life, and garbage from international ships. The mystery of the origin of this varied detritus is surpassed only by that of the waves themselves. Rollers that have the strength to smash logs into oblivion also have the agility to place lightbulbs and Japanese glass fishing floats intact amidst the stones.

To view these beaches from the water, return past the recreation site. A bumpy road parallels the beach for 4 km (2.5 mi) to an old logging camp and boat ramp. A group of five islands and several islets appear like a peninsula from shore. These islands form a protected harbour big enough for most boats. Shallower water between the islands hides numerous rocks and shoals. But with a chart in hand, it's safe to explore among them by canoe or small skiff.

These islands host a tremendous variety of intertidal life. Check tide tables for low tides — two hours later than Prince Rupert on Pacific Daylight Savings Time. Living organisms cover virtually every square centimetre of rock. Edible blue mussels are so numerous they sometimes completely envelop the rocks. Within an area the size of your boat you can see hundreds of sea stars. As you stare into the clear depths, rock scallops' orange lips grin back, and flashes of silver reveal schools of needlefish fleeing for cover.

In calm weather, cruise out past the islands. Bald Eagles seem to escort you toward the horizon. The mountains behind form the northern Queen Charlotte Range. On a calm day, the reflected vistas beg to be photographed. Fishermen seek the twenty fathom (40 m or 120 ft) zone to jig for cod, salmon, and halibut. For variety, try collecting abalone during zero tides along the outer shores. To round out the day, head for the quiet retreat of Gospel Island. As well as a sun-splashed beach, you may discover sea lions and seals basking on its western edge.

The west coast of the Charlottes has a deserved reputation of being wild and unpredictable. Thundering waves and howling winds delight some people, while others prefer a calm sea with gentle breezes. Rennell Sound mirrors all these attributes. A day or two spent on the Pacific side of the islands will give you a feel for their wilder side.

8. Yakoun River and Estuary

Getting There

The community of Port Clements lies within sight of the Yakoun River, which flows into the southern end of Masset Inlet. The river is reached easily at three locations. A partially-paved road leads southward from Port toward Juskatla, paralleling its estuary for 3 km (1.8 mi). A few minutes' drive past the Golden Spruce pullout, the road passes over the Yakoun. Here you can fish the river both up and downstream.

Driving the main backroad north from Charlotte, upstream portions of the river are again easily accessible to the angler. At kilometre 22.3 (14 mi), the gravel road crosses the tea-coloured Yakoun River on a wooden bridge. MacMillan Bloedel maps should be used from here to locate branch roads and river tributaries.

MacMillan Bloedel Limited owns these logging roads. Before driving past Juskatla or up from Charlotte during weekdays between 7:00 a.m. and 5:30 p.m., you must report to their offices for authorization. However, the road between Port Clements and Juskatla is open anytime.

> MacMillan Bloedel Limited:
> Juskatla office (604) 557-4212
> Charlotte shop (604) 559-4224

The Yakoun River is the largest river on the Queen Charlottes. It flows from Yakoun Lake, crossing tree farms and lowlands before emptying into Masset Inlet. The river is important for more than its size, however. The Yakoun provides spawning grounds for all five species of Pacific salmon, and supports a world-famous run of steelhead trout. The drainage of the Yakoun also encompasses the largest watershed and creates the largest estuary on the islands. Estuaries of this size are uncommon on the Charlottes, so this area of mud flat and meadows provides an important feeding ground for wildlife and waterfowl.

The Yakoun's estuary stretches 3 km (1.8 mi) from the

71

Yakoun River and Estuary

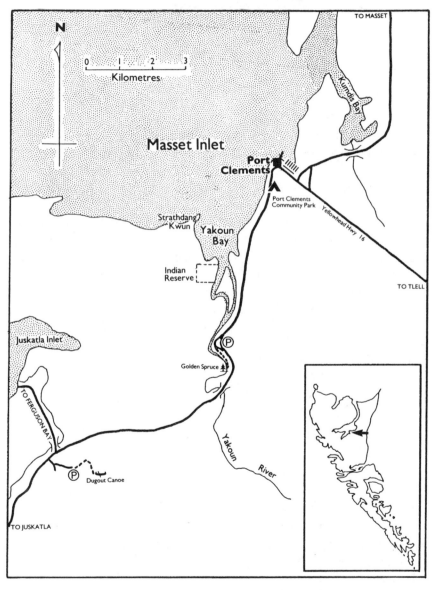

This delta of sediment is where the Yakoun River empties into Masset Inlet. The meeting of fresh and salt water creates valuable habitat for fish, birds and mammals. Upstream changes have substantial effect on these creatures.

government dock at Port Clements to the topographic point of Strathdang Kwun. From the dock the breadth and width of the estuary is evident at low tide. (Try setting crab traps off this dock if you have time.) For a closer inspection of the estuary, follow Bayview Drive from Port Clements south towards Juskatla. Along this stretch you will find several places to park. Some pullouts have easy access to the water's edge through light scrub.

Emerging from the trees at low tide, you walk directly onto a pungent mud flat which stretches to the edge of Masset Inlet. At the high tide line a broad perimeter of knee-high grass conceals the river emerging from the trees. Shallow channels partition the flats and upturned stumps dot the landscape. Although you can see most of the estuary from the estuary edge, gumboots or waders are necessary to cross most channels.

This muddy no-man's land links terrestial, fresh water and marine habitats. The flushing action of the river and ocean brings a continuous supply of nutrients which are stored in the mud. This natural fertilizer accounts for the lush vegetation and presence of many migratory birds.

Thousands of ducks, geese, swans, and shorebirds gather here during migration. They stop briefly to preen, feed, and rest. Others such as swans stay longer, even through the winter. An abundance of plant, animal, and insect food guarantees a continual and varied food supply.

Dabbling ducks such as Mallards frequent these shallows. They

A Great Blue Heron (*Ardea herodias*) stalks frogs, small fish and even mice. It is always alert and wary of man. Herons are not related to Sandhill Cranes, which they resemble. Both species breed on the Queen Charlottes.

feed on plants by 'turning turtle' or grazing on the exposed flats. When alarmed, they lift off with a chorus of quacking and flapping. Diving ducks are distinguished by quite different habits. They prefer deeper water where they dive for fish, molluscs, and intertidal organisms. Although colourful close up, goldeneyes, scaups, buffleheads and scoters all appear black and white at a distance. They require a long taxi across the water to become airborne.

At low tide try wading out to where the waterfowl feed. Streaking ripples in the dark water indicate fish seeking shelter from their enemies. Watch for diving Belted Kingfishers and Great Blue Herons waiting patiently for a fin to break the surface. In summer Sandhill Cranes join the hunt. Two or three of these long-legged waders regularly feed along the water's edge.

Fishing can be as productive for humans. On these islands only the Yakoun contains all five species of eastern Pacific salmon. The Haida have a food fishery for sockeye salmon, which migrate to Yakoun Lake during the spring and early summer. Dilapidated houses, visible at the estuary edge, are occupied by natives during this run. The Yakoun's sport fishery, however, has given this river its national reputation.

Sport fishing on the Yakoun is best late in the year. In early October, five to ten thousand coho begin to move upstream to spawn. These hard-fighting fish gather in pools, near log jams, and through fast water. The river narrows in many places, so casting to the opposite bank isn't difficult. Even so, most anglers wear waders for easier access to their favourite spots.

Steelhead fishing surpasses even the sport for salmon on the Yakoun, and keen residents keep their weekends free from November through January. This highly-prized sport fish "beats the water into a white froth" in the words of one local addict. Catches averaging five to eight kg, with the occasional fish exceeding 9 kg (20 lb), support his claim that the Yakoun has the best steelhead fishing on the islands. Though few reach record size, there are plenty of them, and fewer restrictions apply than on other popular B.C. rivers.

Easy access to the lower end of the Yakoun exists from the Golden Spruce trail and the Yakoun River bridge. You can walk the river banks in both directions and wade shallow riffles in several places. Since the water is tea-coloured, have spare single hook lures such as Spin-n-glows or small silver spoons handy since you may loose them on submerged logs. To fish above the bridge requires considerable driving and knowledge of the roads. Obtain a MacMillan Bloedel map before attempting to fish upstream portions of the river.

Extensive portions of the river are choked with deadfall. One 6 km (3.7 mi) stretch has over twenty-four log jams. The river is navigable by motor boat only on its lowest portion. Check the lower end from the bank before trying to float it. Canoes or small boats can be launched from the small government dock at the base of Tingley Street in Port Clements. There is also a high water launch off a side road at the end of the pavement going towards Juskatla. The view from the water gives an entirely different perspective of this broad salt marsh. On the water you can approach seals and waterfowl, troll for salmon, or set a crab trap while you cruise.

Whether by boat or on foot, expect to have an enjoyable day along any part of the Yakoun River. We wish you tight lines and dry feet!

9. A Charlottes Rainforest

Getting There

A typical temperate rainforest and an unusual spruce can be found 6.3 km (4 mi) south of the Port Clements government dock en route to Juskatla. Drive the gravel road to a pull-out indicated by a sign about the Golden Spruce. A ten minute level trail leads through the woods to end on the Yakoun River. See map, page 72.

Walking into a west coast rainforest can be like entering a religious enclave. Sounds are muffled and the air is cool. The maze of trunks create cloisters where one steps in solemn humility. The buttressed wooden pillars taper up to a fresco of green needles and bright sky. On a sunny day shafts of sunlight may penetrate the lower darkness like beams through a stained-glass window. Tapestries of lichen droop from lower limbs. A thick carpet of moss mantles logs as massive as the tombs of respected statesmen. Such green cathedrals have caused the Charlottes to be nominated "moss capital of Canada."

The feeling of tranquility that pervades the rainforest is mirrored by the soft colours of forest flowers. Exquisite white blossoms of single delight poke shyly just above the forest floor. In contrast, pink spikes of spotted coral-root rise boldly. Coral-root lacks leaves and green chlorophyll which manufacture food in most plants. Nor has coral-root true roots. With assistance from soil fungi the plant draws its sustenance from decayed organic material in the humus. It has adapted well to the low light conditions of this wet temperate forest. As little as ten percent of the available sunlight reaches the forest floor in such a mature forest.

Such dimness, as well as the dense growth and height of these trees are typical of climax rainforests the world over. If this were a tropical climate, the plants would be called jungle, and would be inhabited by hundreds of species of animals, amphibians, reptiles, and birds. A temperate rainforest doesn't have such species variety or abundance, but it shares a similar rainfall.

76

In the rainforest at Ain River on Masset Inlet, hanging gardens of old-man's beard lichen, licorice fern and moss droop from branches. Dying trees sprout shelves of bracket fungus, a sign of internal decay.

The high level of moisture and consequent lack of fire make windthrows and vegetative decay the primary mechanisms of recycling in this forest. Even before a tree falls it is attacked by insects and fungi, helping break it down to basic nutrients for the sustenance of other species. The moss, ferns, lichens, and seedlings that sprout from toppled giants draw their nutrition from the wood even before it becomes soil. These horizontal trunks are aptly named "nurse logs." Sometimes you find a tall tree raised off the ground by its roots as though doing one-handed push-ups. Once it would have been anchored in a nurse log which has since been reduced to soil. Perhaps it was even the offspring of the log which nursed it to maturity.

The species that rise around you are Sitka spruce, western hemlock and western redcedar. Spruce are largest, and have loose scaly bark. These sharp-needled evergreens thrive near salt water where soil is deep and well-drained. Cedars have strips of soft brown bark, and typically grow at low elevations. Hemlock can be identified by furrowed bark which forms scaly ridges. Hemlock is both prolific and shade tolerant, so you will find its seedlings most numerous among the taller trunks. All are engaged in a race for supremacy, to win a place in the canopy above where they can produce the cones that will ensure their own reproduction.

Large trees and their associated flora and fauna dominated British Columbia's coast for millennia before realization of their commercial potential. These giants are still unequalled in size or grandeur anywhere in this country. But the trees of which logging legends are told are increasingly difficult to find. This grove was

Growing on an old stump, this conifer's roots are being exposed as the supporting wood rots. Lack of support will eventually topple the tree, but if it has reproduced, its own seedlings will rise to fill its place.

saved because it aged to the point of being a "cellulose cemetery." That derisive term is used for old-growth trees of no harvestable value. Diseased and rotten, they are viewed by some as valueless despite being the climax of a fully-balanced ecosystem. Many of the trees around you go over 40 m (132 ft) in height. Elsewhere on the islands, trees of even larger size — some with ages approaching a thousand years — have been measured.

In the future trees of this size may rarely grow outside of parks since logging companies intend to cut second growth forests at eighty years of age. British Columbia forest economist Peter Pearse predicts that, if cutting continues at the present rate, the last of B.C.'s old-growth forests will be gone by 2000 A.D. Already only two percent of our forests have large spruce left in them. Somewhat ironically, this places us in a situation similar to those lesser developed countries which are presently being faulted for rapidly clearing their rainforests with disastrous environmental consequences.

Though some of our trees are being replanted, the replacement forests on the Charlottes will never resemble magnificent virgin growth. Cedars will be practically non-existent in second-growth forests because introduced deer eat their seedlings. In fact, cedars are rarely replanted due to their low survival rate. While protective covers help, they are most often too expensive and labour-intensive to be worthwhile. Where the occasional natural cedar struggles above these browsing machines, its home will be logged before the tree reaches a size useful for totem or canoe carving. Browsing deer are even eliminating the cedars that replace those dying a natural death in unlogged stands. Who would have thought that such an unobtrusive animal might have such a potentially severe impact on Haida culture?

The unique golden spruce at the end of this trail is the result of a genetic mutation. Sunlight is normally an essential ingredient for green plants, but is detrimental in this case. The chlorophyll needed for photosynthesis (the process of food manufacture) is mysteriously missing from the leaves. Direct sunlight actually destroys most of the green chlorophyll, leaving yellow as the dominant colour. Forest researchers have grafted limbs of the golden spruce onto other Sitka spruce. They found that in deep shade that branch returns to its normal green colour, but in the sun, goes yellow again. You can easily observe this phenomenon right here. Binoculars allow you to see that the outer needles are yellow, while the inner shaded ones are more natural. The golden colour is best photographed on a sunny morning.

According to Jim Pojar, B.C. forest ecologist, this is the only golden spruce. As logging opens more areas throughout the islands, discoveries of other golden trees have been reported. So far none of these have been substantiated. Most likely the reported sightings have been the result of honest mistakes, as hemlock and spruce can appear yellow under certain conditions. Fortunately the 300-year-old spruce before you was saved from logging.

Large Sitka spruce are prized for their valuable wood. Tall and straight, they have the greatest strength-to-weight ratio of any wood in the world. This made the material invaluable during both world wars when it was used in the manufacture of aircraft, such as the Canadian Mosquito bombers, which flew over Europe. Nowadays spruce is used to make beautiful musical instruments and furniture. Instrument manufacturers prize select specimens without knots and with even grain for guitars and piano sounding boards. Longer lengths are used for frames of furniture since the wood is light and doesn't twist.

This vertical mosaic of undisturbed rainforest is but a small example of the even taller timber which once covered the Charlottes. Big virgin stands are increasingly difficult to reach, so this trail provides an easy way for the road traveller to envision what once was considered an inexhaustible forest.

10.   Of Canoes and Culture

Getting There

The two canoes discussed in this chapter are found in separate locations. You'll find them more interesting if you visit in the sequence described.

The oldest existing Haida canoe found on the Charlottes is located just off the gravel road between Port Clements and Juskatla. This canoe was abandoned before completion, and remains only partly shaped from a huge redcedar. From the museum in Port, drive 14.8 km (9.2 mi) towards Juskatla to a sideroad 0.3 km (0.2 mi) past the Ferguson Bay junction. A sign on the left indicates the sideroad that leads to the canoe. Within 0.3 km is the trailhead, but since turning space there is limited, we advise parking soon after turning onto the sideroad. This is particularly important for large RVs and vehicles with trailers. From the trailhead a five minute walk via a dilapidated bridge and overgrown trail leads to the canoe.

The finished canoe that you should compare this with is stored in a building adjacent to the Queen Charlotte Islands Museum at Skidegate. If you're really keen, you can paddle it by signing on one of the tours of South Moresby conducted by the Haida Gwaii Watchmen.

All tribes of the Pacific Northwest built dugout canoes; these craft were the standard of transportation and were essential for trade, hunting and fishing, and for conducting raids. Haida canoes were prized up and down the coast for their craftsmanship, size, and seaworthiness. The moist climate of the Queen Charlotte Islands produced superior cedar for building the largest canoes, and the Haida's seamanship in open waters gave them dominance over rival tribes. Other tribes were unwilling to attack them in their homeland since the Haida had a tremendous reputation for ferocity and were well-protected by the difficult crossing. The very sight of their war canoes struck terror into tribes as far south as Puget Sound in Washington state. The Haida also had a respected reputation as shrewd traders, and carved canoes for barter as well as for their own use.

Until recently, the last big canoe carved on the Charlottes was in 1909 when Alfred and Robert Davidson were commissioned to build one 17 metres (57 ft) long for the Alaska-Yukon-Pacific Exposition in Seattle, Washington. That giant eventually sold to the National Museum of Canada in Ottawa, Ontario. It was again on display in the Canadian pavilion during Expo '86 in Vancouver, B.C.

Such a canoe could carry 4.5 tonnes (5 tons) of weight. In his 1872 travelogue, Francis Poole tells of travelling from the Charlottes to Victoria in a canoe containing three dozen people. *Queen Charlotte Islands: A Narrative of Discovery and Adventure in the North Pacific* recounts a three week journey on which native paddlers demonstrated phenomenal stamina and skill. That story, and accounts by Rev. William Collison of crossing Hecate Strait in severe weather, will convince even the hardiest river canoeists that whitewater paddling is mere play. Every trip for a Haida had life-threatening risk.

At one time the carving of canoes was an important occupation. The Haida made various sizes during the winter, then paddled them to the mainland each spring for trade. Their success in this commerce was due in part to the size and quality of the cedars which grow in these temperate rainforests. The natives made virtually everything from this soft straight-grained conifer. Hilary Stewart's book *Cedar* aptly calls it the "tree of life," and explains how the Indians selected, cut, and shaped the trunks into canoes.

Evidence of this activity is all over the islands. One important location is Masset Inlet on Graham Island. Villagers from Old Massett went there in January to fall trees as the wood had little sap at that season. Old cedars frequently rot, so the natives sounded the trunks by pounding on them to hear whether they were suited for canoes or house construction. Once a suitable candidate was found, a test hole might be cut to the heartwood to confirm its soundness. If solid, the tree would be felled after an appropriate ceremony. Logs destined to become canoes would be rough-shaped on site before being towed back to the village.

After European diseases ravaged entire villages, and manufactured boats became available, such labours were abandoned. Brush eventually concealed all evidence of the old logging. In recent decades hikers and loggers have encountered stumps, tree-tops, and even unfinished blanks forgotten in the woods. Several such blanks can be seen in Masset Inlet, but the most accessible is in an old clear-cut near Port Clements. The bow of that unfinished canoe faces the stump

81

from which it was felled. That canoe is fully 3 km (2 mi) from the nearest beach. The job of dragging the cured and hollowed hull through the forest would be done by slaves and hired men who specialized in canoe carving. The final shaping, steam-spreading, and painting would take place back at the village.

Scores of dugouts were once drawn up on the beach before Skidegate Village. At low tide canoe runs are still visible on its southern edge of the beach. These are paths perpendicular to the shore where cleared beach stones allowed canoes to land and launch without damage to the bottom.

Until recently it had been more than a century since the challenge of canoe construction had been undertaken by craftsmen of Skidegate. Then the Bank of British Columbia commissioned one for exhibition at Expo '86. Designer and construction foreman was the acclaimed artist Bill Reid, whose hometown is Skidegate. The completion of his 18 m (59 ft) craft despite inter-personal tensions and woodwork problems is chronicled in a video shown in the Queen Charlotte Islands Museum. Rediscovery of forgotten techniques were crucial in the execution of this immense project. Haida are justifiably proud of *Loo Taas* — meaning Wave Eater. It is symbolic of their renewed tribal vigor.

On July 11th, 1987 *Loo Taas* arrived in Skidegate after several crews spent three weeks paddling it back from Vancouver. It had attracted little attention on the waters at the fair, but 2000 people crowded the beach as it swept toward its ancestral home. The sun was bright that emotional day. At a distance no paddlers could be distinguished, but the flash of synchronous paddles telegraphed the canoe's progress. Closer, ten bare-chested men drove pointed paddles forward and back to the beat of a tambourine drum. *Loo Taas* spat an impressive bow wake. The paddlers' deep 'oooh-ah' chant resonated cross the water. Bill Reid sat in the stern before the steersman, a blue fedora shielding his proud face. How his heart must have throbbed to that chorus!

That night Skidegate gave a potlatch at which a thousand guests sat down for dinner. The feasting, singing, dancing, oratory, and gift-giving made that evening the event of the decade on the islands. The ceremony will be a life-long memory for all of us who attended. That such canoes are worthy of regional and national recognition indicates the value of Haida heritage for all Canadians. We hope *Loo Taas* will gnash these waters for years to come.

11. Nadu: Trails to Tribulation

Getting There

Nadu Road is marked on Yellowhead Highway No. 16 about halfway between Port Clements and Masset, approximately 19 km (11.8 mi) north of Port Clements. From the pavement a 2.3 km gravel road ends at Masset Sound. Due to limited turning area, no trailers or large RVs should attempt this road. If possible, time your visit with a falling tide.

On Masset Sound at the end of Nadu Road are two short walks which graphically illustrate the broken dreams found in so many places on these islands. Here moulder the failed remnants of a homestead and of a business enterprise. Overgrown pioneer settlements and abandoned industrial sites are the major marks of white men throughout the Charlottes. The easy access to two such ventures at Nadu is a way of getting the feel of many in just a couple of hours.

The side road into Nadu was originally built during the 1920s to supply subsistence farmers inland from the water's edge. The highway did not exist then, so transportion was by steamship.

The road's slope near the sound was logged in the 1970s and is an opportunity for those who haven't travelled the backroads to see a clear-cut. New hemlock trees are growing rapidly to cover this scar. Their phenomenal growth rate has already concealed much evidence of the tribulations civilization has put to this landscape.

Gumboots are mandatory footgear for both Nadu locations. You reach a rock breakwater at the homestead by following the shoreline south from the dock where you park. For easiest walking, be certain to begin your journey about two hours after high tide and return before it comes in! Don't forget to add two hours to the Prince Rupert tables for accurate timing since you're on enclosed Masset Inlet. Overhanging vegetation makes the shoreline traverse very difficult during high tide.

Within 1 km (0.5 mi) you reach an unmortared breakwater built of beach cobbles. The even sides and attention to design are marks of a skilled stonemason. After seven decades only a small portion

Nadu

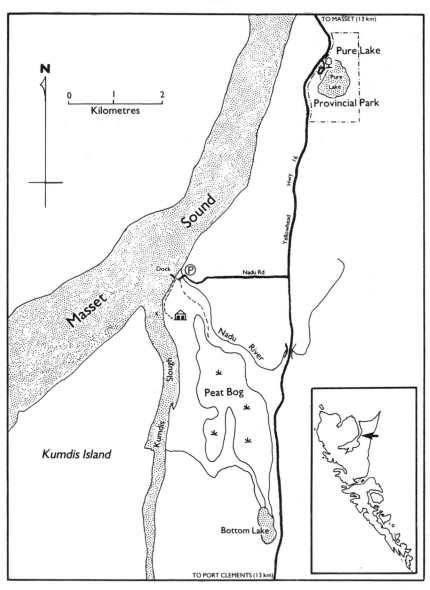

Stone breakwater and boat ramp at Nadu. This homestead is remarkable for the quality construction still evident in all of its structures. All farms which were attempted on Masset Inlet eventually failed.

has collapsed. This labour of love is rarely seen among modern homesteaders and indicates the care put into all the construction on this site.

Follow a trail up the embankment behind the collapsed boathouse. This leads through the cedars to a clearing with a 'fruitless' apple orchard. In 1911 the promising new home of the Edward Evans family stood here. The three huge rhododendron bushes give evidence to his wife's efforts to domesticate the wilderness. These transplanted southern shrubs have reached 6 m (20 ft) in height and display gorgeous blooms during the first week of July.

The smooth adze marks on the collapsed house beams and the even joints are obviously the mark of an artist. We immediately suspected that a Scandinavian lived here. Later we read in Dalzell's *The Queen Charlotte Islands, 1774 -1966* that "master axemen" Ole Anderson and Alec Johnson were engaged by Evans to build this substantial house.

The craftsmanship and aesthetic touches devoted to this homestead only serve to enhance the sense of despair that pervades the place — so much for naught. It must have been devastating to leave these dreams and dollars behind. This is a story typical of Charlottes farming. Encouraged by exaggerated agricultural claims and government land give-aways, many pioneers devoted everything they had to their farms. Today no one on the islands earns a living solely from crops or cattle.

Oddly, many back-to-the-landers ignored this history when they immigrated to the Charlottes in the late 60s and 70s. Not only were these latter-day pioneers weak in their sense of history, but they also lacked the strong work ethic of their forebears. Most squatted on the land (held no property title) and sought only to eke a living. It wasn't enough. Like Nadu, virtually all their communities, some on remote islands, have been abandoned. A creeping layer of green overtakes them all.

In 1967 another enterprise started at Nadu with the same high hopes that possessed previous pioneers. Bering Industries of Victoria, B.C. spent a million dollars constructing a peat moss plant for the processing of a nearby bog into a horticultural product. The moss was extracted by draining the bog, allowing the dry top layer of moss to be suctioned off.

Ironically, the very factors that make peat useless for farming are excellent when the moss is added to proper soil. Its sterility, lightness, compressibility, absorptive nature, and organic composition make it easy to work with and useful for gardening and other purposes.

You can follow an alder-grown road up a gentle incline to the bog workings about 1.6 km (1 mi) away. The walk passes through a mixed wood to a bench above Nadu River. There are no views until the trees give way at the edge of the bog. Little remains at the extraction site, but if you haven't visited a bog before, this is a good opportunity to do so.

The reason for the failure of this peat business is unclear, although the distance to markets must have been a factor. Peat harvesting operations in the lower Fraser Valley would be more competitive in this regard. Evidently only one shipment was made from this facility. Only the foundations of the buildings and a slowly rotting dock remain from this venture.

Of all the efforts to earn a living attempted on these islands, only fishing and logging have met with continued success. As we learn more of the importance of careful management of our so-called renewable resources, even their future is uncertain. But the land itself of the Queen Charlotte Islands offers a new opportunity; one which is just beginning to develop — tourism. With international attention now focused on the adventure of touring these beautiful islands, the potential for the non-exploitive use of the area's natural attributes has developed. Here at last is an enterprise which can maintain and enhance the independent lifestyle so cherished by islanders. We hope this new industry will be successful.

12. Langara Island Vicinity

Getting There

Though the location is remote, it's possible for the venturesome to organize their own travel and camp at Langara Island. Floatplanes and possibly a fishing boat can be chartered out of Masset. Camping locations are Cape Knox and Lepas or Pillar Bays on Graham Island, but avoid staying on Indian reserves. Mooring buoys for yachters are located in Pillar Bay, Bruin Bay (3), Henslung Cove (3), Beal Cove (4), Cloak Bay (3), and three in front of Kiusta (beware of the nasty reef).

Called North Island by some, Langara is a forested low-profile rocky isle about 25 sq km (10 sq mi) in area. Lying off the northwestern tip of Graham Island, it's fully exposed to the pounding Pacific. Wind, waves, and a serrated shore give it a frightening sort of beauty. The scenery is memorable, but you wouldn't want to get into any trouble out here. This location is too remote for drop-in visitors, yet has attracted an interesting variety of people. Over the centuries these have included Haida villagers, trading sailors, fishermen, environmental students, lighthouse keepers, and biologists.

Originally the Haida lived around the island in several villages, the largest being Kiusta on nearby Graham Island. This site was abandoned about 1850 when most of the residents migrated to the Alaskan panhandle and eastward toward Masset. Kiusta has been used only seasonally since, yet native use of this area is long-standing. In 1986 archeologists from the Queen Charlotte Islands Museum uncovered campfire charcoal which was subsequently dated back 10,400 years. If verified by further investigation, this will be one of the oldest known sites of human activity in British Columbia. Such long-standing aboriginal colonization makes early hit and miss 'discoveries' of the Charlottes by European navigators seem like a game of peek-a-boo.

English fur trader George Dixon was the first European to

Langara Island

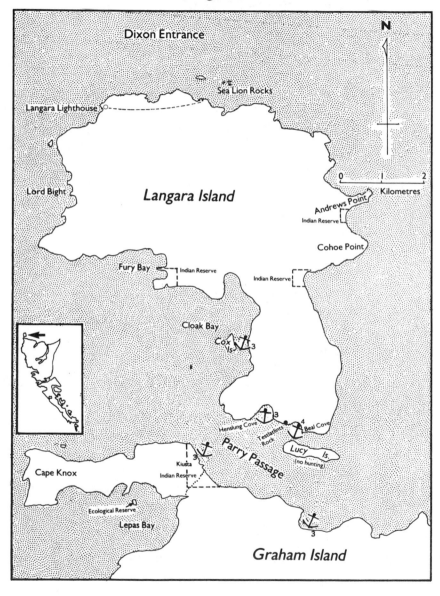

Langara angler shows his spring salmon. These fish can grow over 45 kg (100 lbs) and are eagerly sought by sport and commercial fishermen. The former call a fish over 13.5 kg (30 lbs) a tyee, the latter call them smilies.

circumnavigate this archipelago in 1787. He named it after Queen Charlotte, wife of George III of England. He also named Langara North Island, and Cloak Bay after this profitable exchange: "There were ten canoes about the ship, which contained, as nearly as I could estimate, 120 people; many of these brought most beautiful beaver cloaks, others excellent skins, and, in short, none came empty handed, and the rapidity with which they sold them was a circumstance additionally pleasing; they fairly quarreled with each other about which should sell his cloak first . . . " These were the glory days for the sea otter trade which nearly put this marine mammal into extinction.

One resource with a continuing abundance at Langara Island is fish. Superlative salmon catches in this vicinity have been known to the commercial fleet for years. Now the lucrative sports fishing industry has discovered the area as well. In 1985 a floating lodge was anchored in Henslung Cove for fly-in clients. One patron declared this world class experience as "The best fishing I've had in thirty years on the B.C. coast." Current weight records at Langara Lodge stand at 51.3 kilograms (114 pounds) for halibut, 34.2 kg (76 lbs) for spring salmon, and 10.1 kg (22.5 lbs) for the largest coho salmon landed. Large ling cod and chum salmon supplement the take. The lodge has gained a far-reaching reputation and capacity bookings as a result of such tremendous catches. Several other floating resorts have since joined it. All these operations are relatively expensive and open to reserved guests only. Their booking offices are located in

Vancouver and Victoria, and are advertised in international fishing periodicals and the *Saltwater Fishing Guide*, available free from Travel Infocentres throughout the province.

In contrast to such modern accommodation, adolescents who participate in a program called Rediscovery live closer to the land. These island teens use rustic cabins at Lepas Bay as their base. Each summer consecutive two-week programs involve hands-on learning to create environmental awareness, outdoor skills, and respect for traditional Haida culture. Rediscovery has been so successful that the originators have given training workshops for instructors in the United States.

The lightkeepers on Langara Island are the only people who live on the island year-round. Langara light is notoriously difficult for boat landing, as there's no moorage, and most people come and go by helicopter. They serve us all by manning directional beacons, and taking weather and seismograph (earthquake) readings. Since submarine earthquakes sometimes generate tsunamis (destructive marine waves), this lighthouse is the vanguard of the Canadian early warning system. The station was established in 1913 at the same time as its companion on the southern tip of this island chain — Cape St. James.

Like their rocky counterpart, Cape Knox and Lepas Bay on Graham Island are completely exposed. Both also provide plenty of rugged scenery. Cape Knox also offers the possibility of cave exploration. Out from Pillar Bay's beach facing Dixon Entrance towers a 29 m (95 ft) column of conglomerate rock. There are similar though smaller features in Cloak Bay; one called Porthole Rock has a 2 m (6 ft) hole through it.

Another geological oddity is Plum Pudding Rock, or Testatlints, in Parry Passage. This enormous boulder, accessible at low tide, is topped by a thicket of trees and sits on the shore of Langara Island. Recognized by geologists as an erratic, it was deposited by glaciers during the Ice Age. A shaman whose grave is on its summit gave the stone his name.

Walking about on land is the way to really appreciate these locations. Just within the trees at Kiusta, a row of depressions outlines the location of houses in the former village. Only a few corner posts remain upright to mark their perimeter. Roof beams covered in moss lie across the pits, and the rainforest crowds close, a scene typical of abandoned Haida sites. What is unusual here is a

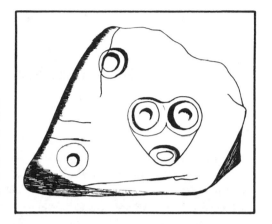

Petroglyphs on a beach boulder at Kiusta. The age and purpose of such rock carvings are unknown. Three-dimensional petroglyphs are not the same as pictographs, or rock paintings. The latter are not found on the Charlottes.

three-pole mortuary which once supported the remains of a Haida chief. Called the Edenshaw pole, this triple totem is the only one of its kind in existence. At the far end of the beach behind it, faces stare from rocks at the tide line. The meaning and function of such petroglyphs are unknown as they were rarely chipped by the Haida.

A trail leads across the wooded peninsula from Kiusta to the famous crescent beach at Lepas Bay. A spectacular fifty-five km (35 mi) coastal hike begins here. The route south encounters caves and misty rainforest, beachcombing treasures and fresh water fishing. Sea-run cutthroat trout can attain sporting size in coastal creeks with steady flows.

Any visit to Langara Island would be incomplete without seeing its Peregrine Falcons. These streamlined hunters are admired the world over for their speed and flight finesse. At one time the population here was phenomenally dense; up to twenty pairs nested on the cliffs. Since 1968 only five to seven nests have been active. Pesticides which were subsequently banned or perhaps changes in ocean currents which diminished their food supply may be partially to blame. But recent research has faulted black rats, an introduced pest common in the Charlottes.

Despite the remoteness of Langara, civilization has upset its cultural and biological balance. Much was lost before we could slow progress to understand and appreciate this place. But like a forgiving mother, Langara Island still offers us her beauty, her resources, and her spirit. Knowing now her delicacy, we must act responsibly to preserve and even restore the natural attributes we damaged in our delinquency.

13. Delkatla Wildlife Sanctuary

Getting There

This 553 ha (1382 a) lowland refuge lies adjacent to the village of Masset on Masset Sound. Delkatla is accessible by car and trail, and has viewing towers. To visit, follow Tow Hill Road east past the causeway, then turn left on Cemetery Road and drive 1.7 km (1.1 mi) to a gravel parking lot. Begin your walk at this location or along the dike, 300 m (328 yds) farther.

The Masset-Haida Lions Club runs a campsite across from the refuge, between the causeway and Cemetery Road. Partial hookups, a wash house, showers, and kitchen shelter are available. The Travel Infocentre near the causeway has a free sani-station.

Every spring millions of shorebirds and waterfowl leave their wintering areas and fly north to nesting grounds in the Arctic. One route they follow lies along the western edge of North America — the Pacific Flyway. Birds can't make such trip without stopping for rest, shelter, and food, so favourite locations spaced along their flyways meet these temporary requirements. Delkatla slough is one such habitat, and is one of the best places on the Charlottes to see birds during spring migration, as well as in the fall when they return.

The sanctuary's marsh is bordered by Masset townsite, roads, and a border of dense conifers. Several ponds of varying sizes, separated by ditches and dikes, cover most of the sanctuary. The tide floods the basin irregularly through a gate in the causeway, over which runs the road to Masset. The gate was installed in 1977 to permit the saltwater flushing necessary to keep trees from growing in the meadows. Water levels on the largest pond now fluctuate, revealing extensive mud flats following low tides. Above the water line, lush grass, wildflowers, and small trees grow in the dark soil. Birds use all these habitats.

A short trail from the parking area along Cemetery Road leads to a viewing tower. This is an excellent vantage from which to scan the entire marsh with binoculars, but the best birding begins as you return to ground level. Three trails lead to the waterways. Bird Walk

Delkatla Wildlife Sanctuary

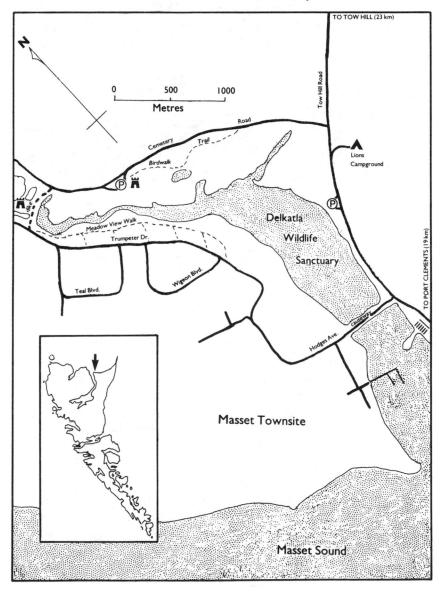

Male Northern Pintail ducks (*Anas acuta*). These are non-diving ducks, so require shallow water in which to feed. They breed and reside year-round on the Charlottes.

Trail is marked by a driftwood sign at the Cemetery Road parking lot and winds pleasantly along the treed side of the refuge. Rustic benches provide an opportunity to sit quietly listening for calls. Through the dark foliage you may glimpse a shy Varied Thrush or chatty Winter Wren. This border should also be searched for a Steller's Jay or Hairy Woodpecker. Particular subspecies of these birds are endemic to these islands.

At several spots the trail emerges at meadows and ponds. Skulk along the edge of a ditch, staying alert for waterfowl. Fanfares of untuned trumpets will announce the arrival of the largest — swans and geese. Mallards, American Wigeons, and teal may be feeding with their tails turned up in the shallows. They can execute near-vertical take-offs, which allows them into confined ponds and ditches. A Bald Eagle or Peregrine Falcon may suddenly appear, causing these prey to scatter. An alarmed Common Snipe may burst out, while Lincoln's Sparrows furtively flit between the grass hummocks.

A second route may be walked or driven along a dike which bisects the marsh. It begins 300 m (325 yd) past the first parking lot on Cemetery Road. Midway along, a second viewing tower provides a platform to set up a spotting scope to observe distant waterfowl. Wade through thigh-high grass near the ponds. This open portion of Delkatla is the best area to see Sandhill Cranes performing their

A dowitcher uses its bill to probe the bottom like a sewing machine, feeding on small invertebrates. These are the only snipe-like shorebirds seen on open mudflats.

spring courtship dance. You'll need patience and stealth to sight these elegant birds leaping repeatedly skyward, then dropping awkwardly to earth, all the while flapping, trumpeting, and bowing.

Sandhill Cranes are but one of 113 species of birds recorded at Delkatla. This high number of sightings is mainly due to the dedication and commitment of local naturalist Margo Hearne. For fourteen years she has recorded migration patterns and numbers, details so important for research on species breeding. Recent studies involved the Least Sandpiper, a tiny shorebird which normally breeds on the Arctic barrens. For unknown reasons up to ninety pairs have nested at Delkatla, currently the highest breeding density in North America. In 1987 adults and downy young were colour banded. By late summer, only the immatures remained. Their parents had left for Central America, leaving the juveniles to find their own way south.

Unfortunately, these and other ground-nesting birds have to contend with obnoxious neighbours. Hereford cattle graze within the sanctuary, as fences are not maintained and offer no resistance to their entry. These lumbering beasts create havoc by disturbing incubating adults and squashing ground nests. Since Delkatla is

95

only a municipal sanctuary, it has no environmental protection.

From Trumpeter Drive at the eastern edge of Masset, Meadow View Walk offers unobstructed views over the open water. In late April and early May, chocolate-coloured dowitchers probe the muck, black-banded Killdeer cry plaintively, and flocks of tiny shorebirds zoom over the water's edge like jets in formation. Over twenty species of shorebirds have been recorded here.

Most birds that stop at Delkatla are normally expected along the Pacific Flyway. But rare species do drop in from unexpected places. A warm-weather Cattle Egret was spotted during one Christmas bird count. Marbled Godwits, normally found east of the Rockies, have also made a surprise appearance. Both these birds are rare in B.C. Since it's on a major migration route, Delkatla will always be a good place for birders to visit. Spring and fall are the best times, but a storm may yield a few surprises. Who knows? You might spot a transient from Siberia or witness the spectacular stoop of a Peregrine Falcon.

Sunset reflects on Tow Hill, North Beach, Naikoon Provincial Park. Composed of basalt columns, the hill is a volcanic sill.

Sunset at Harriet Harbour, southern Queen Charlotte Islands.

A couple of hefty Spring Salmon displayed by guests of Langara Lodge.

Brenda Hatter and companion paddle a Feathercraft collapsible sea kayak.

A Japanese fishing float washes in the spume on South Beach, Graham Island.

Coastal Western Hemlock forest.

Old Man's Beard lichen in rainforest.

Moresby Wilderness Area, southern Queen Charlotte Islands, with tiny Flowerpot Island showing in mid-channel.

The view west from the summit of Tow Hill, Naikoon Provincial Park. Yakan Point in the distance; campground just off the beach.

A quiet evening looking over Juan Perez Sound toward the San Cristoval Range, South Moresby region.

An impressive Sitka Spruce near Windy Bay, Lyell Island.

Sitka Blacktail Deer eating Stinging Nettle.

A very rare opportunity to photograph a pod of Killer Whales on Tar Islands, South Moresby region.

Killer Whale (Orcinus orca).

Ninstints Village mortuary totems, World Heritage Site in South Moresby region.

Mortuary totems, Ninstints Village. Thirty-two poles remain at this site which was abandoned in the 1880s.

Moss-grown Haida skull, Skedans Village, Louise Island.

Chiefs of the Haida Nation wait on the beach for the arrival of the canoe, Loo Taas, at Skidegate Village.

Haida paddlers bring home the dugout canoe, Skidegate Village.

Unloading expedition gear from Grumman "Goose," Hotsprings Island, South Moresby.

104

Introduction to Naikoon Provincial Park

If you've ever stood in wonder before the monumental "Raven and the First Men" in the University of B.C. Museum of Anthropology in Vancouver, you've been touched by Naikoon. This world-famous cedar carving by Haida artist Bill Reid interprets the creation of humans on Rose Spit in Naikoon Provincial Park. That such artistry was inspired here is indicative of the special nature of this landscape.

The boundaries of Naikoon Park contain about 72,600 ha (182,000 a) of beaches, sand dunes, bogs, and lakes. With the exception of two bedrock outcrops, over 100 km (62 mi) of continuous beach form its oceanic perimeter. Here extensive sand deposits are continuously blown into shifting dunes behind the driftwood. The park's interior is largely a boggy lowland interspersed with a few lakes. This is the Argonaut Plain, and all landforms on it have been shaped by glaciers thousands of years ago. Some significant scientific discoveries have been made here, but it is ground of little commercial value.

Amazingly, the provincial government promoted development of this plain by issuing homestead permits during the early 1900s. Although none of those early settlers established permanent residence, private property still exists within today's park boundary. Modern homes along the northern beaches and the Tlell River have replaced the old homesteads.

The British Columbia government made a wiser land-use decision in 1973 when Naikoon Provincial Park was created. A park was an excellent choice for the preservation of this area's landforms and lowland typical of B.C.'s coast. Naikoon also served to protect the habitat of a number of interesting species of plants, birds, and fish. The 50 mm (2 in) threespine stickleback has evolved specialized subspecies in some of the park's lakes. That this area has environmental significance is indicated by three Provincial ecological reserves near the boundaries of the park. The casual visitor, however, is very likely most interested in the park's recreational opportunities. And there are plenty of these!

Naikoon Provincial Park

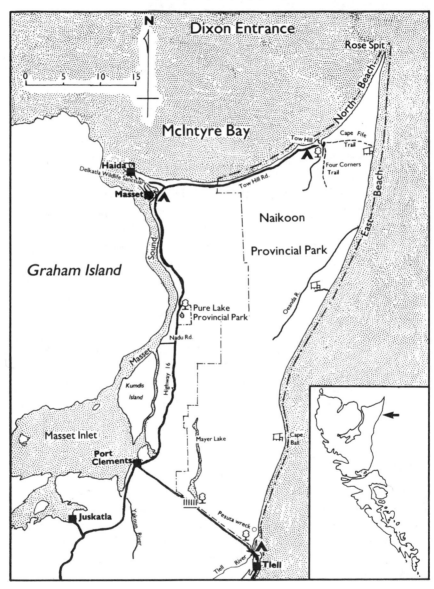

A Haida myth supposes mankind survived the Great Flood within a shell such as these clams on Rose Spit. Other tribes begin their history with a flood. Could their colonizations have coincided with the melting of the Ice Age?

Naikoon has places for everything from speeding beach buggies to quiet nature contemplation. There are forest trails for families, a coastal trek for experienced backpackers, and beachcombing for everyone to enjoy. Fishing draws many anglers, particularly in the fall when salmon and steelhead enter the park's rivers. Both sea-run and resident cutthroat trout can be fished in the Tlell and Sangan Rivers, and in Mayer Lake. Mayer Lake is great for canoeing, and has a ramp for trailered boaters as well.

Other facilities include serviced campsites at the north and south ends of the park. They provide no hot water, hookups, or sani-dumps, but such services are available outside the park. All stores and commercial services are in the nearby villages of Masset or Port Clements. There are picnic areas in a satellite provincial park called Pure Lake, and at Tow Hill, Mayer Lake, and Tlell River, all within Naikoon.

Park headquarters are located on Yellowhead Highway No. 16 just south of the Tlell River. Reservations are not accepted for camping, and a fee is normally charged. A regular licence is required for fishing within provincial parks. Hunting is not permitted in Naikoon from April 1st to September 1st. For brochures and current information, contact the supervisor at:

Naikoon Provincial Park
Box 19
Tlell, B.C. VOT 1YO
Telephone: (604) 557-4390

14. Tow Hill Area

Getting There

From Masset a narrow but well-travelled gravel road leads east past the Canadian Forces base towards Naikoon Provincial Park. It passes beachfront homes and an ecological reserve before reaching Agate Beach Campground at km 23 (mi 14.5). Beyond the campground the road rounds Tow Hill and reaches the access onto North Beach at km 25 (mi 15.7). Trailers are best dropped at the campground before continuing, as there is limited turning space at the hill.

The rounded dome of Tow Hill is the dominant landmark and a must-see for visitors to Naikoon Park. The hill has picnic facilities, a short trail to its summit, and a grand view of Dixon Entrance. From its base anglers may cast into a river or the sea, jig offshore for halibut, or set crab traps beyond the surf. Hiking routes lead inland and in both directions along the extensive beaches. This is a pleasant place to picnic for a few hours, or to linger for a few days of camping and exploration.

Agate Beach Campground has twenty gravel pads, a kitchen shelter, pit toilets, and a hand pump well. The water is discoloured, but safe to drink. Agate Beach is open year-round; an overnight fee is charged May through September. Arrive early to secure a space as the closest alternative is the Lions RV Park in Masset.

Agate Beach is named for the translucent stones found all along this shore. They're a form of quartz and are washed by waves out of glacial deposits, then tumbled in the saltwater swash until they gleam. They aren't precious, but don't try telling this to a child. For young castaways, these are diamonds from a pirate's booty.

The pebble beach gives way to soft sand at low tide. If the surf is down, inflatable boats can be launched from the beach. The water averages four to ten fathoms (24 to 60 ft) deep offshore, ideal for jigging for bottomfish. Buzz Bombs, cod jigs, or baited hooks are popularly used for halibut. If you don't have a boat, try bait-casting for groundfish from the rocky point into the surf. The Hiellen River also produces cutthroat trout and Dolly Varden. Commercial fishermen work offshore for Dungeness crabs, which are abundant.

Tow Hill

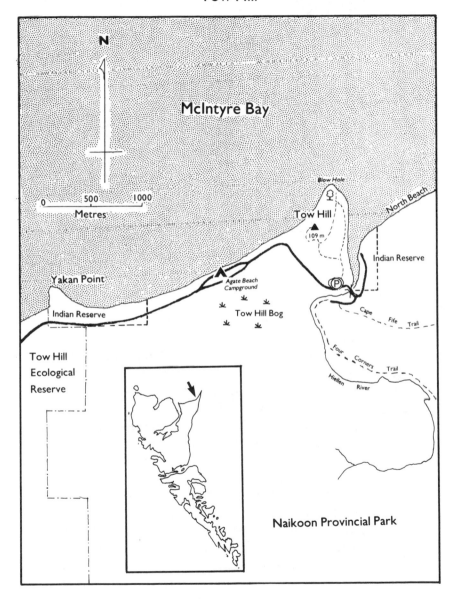

N

McIntyre Bay

0   500   1000
Metres

Blow Hole

Tow Hill

North Beach

109 m

Indian Reserve

Yakan Point

Agate Beach
Campground

P

Indian Reserve

Tow Hill Bog

Cape

Fife

Trail

Tow Hill
Ecological
Reserve

Four

Corners

Trail

Hiellen

River

Naikoon Provincial Park

Fishing in the Hiellen River can be good despite local traffic. Dolly Varden and cutthroat trout are caught in summer, with a small coho run in the fall.

You can set out traps as well.

From the campground Tow Hill is a fifteen minute walk along the beach or a 2 km (1.2 mi) ride along the road. From its ocean side the character of Tow Hill can be studied. The cliff is composed of hexagonal columns of rock which fit together like six-sided cells of honeycomb. This is basalt, an igneous or fire-formed stone, which long ago flowed into cracks of sandstone already in place here. The molten basalt cooled, then cracked into metre-wide columns.

Tow Hill was further shaped by glaciers during the last Ice Age. When viewed from North Beach, it's easy to see the gradual inland slope of the hill compared to its fluted face. As the wall of ice pushed down from the Queen Charlotte Mountains, it deposited gravel against the back side before rising over the hill and moving out to sea. On the seaward side, bedrock was plucked away. This left an excellent example of a landform called a roche moutonne.

The Haida have a creative legend interpreting the formation of several rock features at this location. The story involves an eagle, a whale, and an angry ogre named Tow, evidence of which can be found here today. The myth is recounted in considerable detail by Kathleen Dalzell in her authoritative history *The Queen Charlotte*

Islands — Book 2: Of Places and Names.

From the parking lot at the base of Tow Hill, a trail meanders along the Hiellen River past picnic tables to a rocky point beneath the cliff. A boardwalk branches from the picnic site up to the 109 m (360 ft) summit. On a clear day islands in the Alaskan panhandle can be seen to the north, 72 km (45 mi) across Dixon Entrance. Sickle-shaped North Beach slices the surf on the right. To the left, the campsite, and in the distance beyond, the ridge of the Queen Charlotte Mountains. Directly below the look-out the cliff drops to a rocky point. Pelagic Cormorants gather there before roosting overnight on the cliff face. This edge is concealed — do not leave the established trail!

After appreciating the vistas and crashing surf around the hill, you may want to investigate the forests behind it. Here the pale-flowering beauty of single delight and the whistle of a shy Varied Thrush are contrasting pleasures on a micro scale. Among these trees a general store, post office, and clam cannery once operated. All that remains is a rusting boiler in the trees downstream from the bridge. This property belongs to the Masset Indian Band, and camping is not permitted on it.

In the early 1900s - vast tracts of Graham Island were promoted for agricultural settlement by an ill-informed government in Victoria. Immigrants arrived to locate unsurveyed land which had no access. Neither was there an export market for the produce they grew. At first only a few determined settlers used the beach as their road, but by 1912 there were about a hundred people dealing at the Tow Hill store. World War I and the subsequent Depression ended their efforts. Today their wagon routes are walking trails from Tow Hill to East Beach and the park's interior. To walk them is to gain an appreciation of the work ethic of these pioneers.

The departure point for both the Four Corners and Cape Fife trails is an unmarked sideroad on the immediate east side of the Hiellen River. Vehicles are best left nearby at the Tow Hill parking lot. Neither trail is particularly suited to mountain biking, but can be walked by small children along the initial portions.

The Four Corners trail heads south for 4.8 km (3 mi) along a mossy road which deteriorates into a trail. Saplings crowd closer near Four Corners, but the route is always obvious. Digging the drainage ditches along this access must have been back-breaking labour and their subsequent abandonment heart-rending. Apart from a few fence posts and a rotting bridge, all other signs of former homesteads have disappeared. Gumboots, compass, and 1:50,000 topographic maps are mandatory beyond here.

Take time though to investigate the bogs alongside the road. Here you might surprise a cock-eared deer or even Sandhill Cranes. These birds nest in such places. Occasionally they will be heard overhead, calling with a guttural, vibrating 'gar-oo-oo-oo'. Trumpeter Swans may have once nested nearby, as the names Swan Creek and Cygnet Lake attest. Determined birders might attempt to document definitive evidence as this would be a significant provincial record.

The Cape Fife trail leads to East Beach (see **East Beach** chapter). This trail winds 10 km (6.3 mi) through rainforest and open woods before reaching sand dunes just south of Kumara Lake. The route is level, and in good condition with cedar timbers spanning wet and muddy portions. About the half-way point, the dark woods are left behind as more open marshes and meadows appear. Near km 5 (mi 3) is a wilderness campsite and trailside bench. A flagged route forks over to Mica Lake from here, but there is no ground suited for tenting at this location. Allow fifteen minutes to reach the lake and watch carefully for concealed flagging tape.

The eastern end of the trail is marked by a hiking shelter. A circle trip can be made by following the East and North Beach back to Tow Hill, but this makes an exceedingly long day. Try to have a vehicle pick you up on the North Beach or camp overnight to make this an easier option.

From a base at Agate Beach, the person who is curious about the natural environment or is just seeking quiet relaxation can easily spend three or four days in the Tow Hill vicinity.

15. Tow Hill Bog

Getting There

Proceed 23 km (14.5 mi) from Masset along the road into Naikoon Park. Across the road from Agate Beach Campground, follow deer trails up onto a typical peat bog. Gumboots are necessary. Two minutes of walking will place you in this interesting environment. A good place to get an overall view of this bog can be obtained from the summit of Tow Hill (see preceding chapter).

Bog communities have their own beauty and points of ecological interest, but the landscape and even the name, put some people off. "Who wants to stomp about a sodden swamp?" seems to be their thought. But Canada has more bogs than any other country, and bogs are a major feature of B.C.'s coast, so saving these on the Argonaut Plain was a major reason for this park's creation. In fact, an ecological reserve has been created nearby to give this vegetative resource additional protection for research purposes.

This peaty plain was formed and is maintained by high rainfall and poor drainage. That the water table is close to the surface is shown by numerous small pools. Few plants can tolerate such a root-soaked habitat. Dominant and easily recognized are stunted conifers, evergreen shrubs such as salal, and *Sphagnum* moss. Ten species of this peat-forming moss have been identified here.

The solid strata of moss, capable of filling shallow bodies of water with its growth, functions much like a sponge, and indeed feels like one underfoot. As well as inhibiting the water's flow, and preventing oxygenation, the moss also turns it acidic. It does this by releasing tannin, a natural plant by-product. This chemical accounts for Naikoon's brownish streams. Tannin is also a component of tea. You might consider yourself to be walking across a gigantic tea bag!

Such chemical conditions, typical of peat bogs, are in fact necessary for their development. A bog is defined as a deposit of partially-decomposed organic matter. The *Sphagnum* moss and other plants that grow here are not broken down into soil when they die, as happens in most plant decay. Bacteria and microscopic organisms which normally carry out the task of decomposition are deficient in bogs due to the acid and lack of oxygen. Thus each year's growth is established on layers of previous plants. Bogs often develop many metres deep, and can date back to the end of the Ice Age. Although their lowermost layers become black and oozy, laboratory analysis still reveals the identity of woody pieces and microscopic pollen grains released by flowers each spring. Most pollen is scattered on the ground, so peat bogs function like a bank containing extensive deposits undamaged by decay. Since each species' pollen looks different, scientists can tell what plants once grew in this vicinity.

Researchers recently discovered a species of fir tree which grew here 30,000 years ago. What's even more remarkable is that there are no firs growing naturally on the Charlottes today. They were evidently removed by the ice sheets and have not grown again. Yet this conifer is found on the adjacent northern mainland. In other instances some plants which grow on these islands are found nowhere else in B.C., or have their closest companions in the Orient or Asia. Such unusual distributions, and the changes to our earth's historic climate which they imply, are a subject of considerable debate among scientists.

Additional discoveries in ancient deposits at Cape Ball on East Beach have provided some of the evidence for refugia (ice-free areas) in the Charlottes. For years geologists have refuted suggestions that pockets of green would have survived at low elevations during the Ice Age. Botanists and zoologists have argued otherwise because the odd distribution of plants and subspecies of animals found on the Charlottes is best explained by uninterrupted evolution within a refugium.

The depths of a bog are revealing, so the surface can hardly be dull. Examination on your knees soon demonstrates this. If you visit Tow Hill Bog in early July you'll find two inconspicuous plants in bloom. Even if they're not flowering, the adaptations of the round-leaved sundew and the common butterwort will boggle your mind.

These plants are insectivorous, meaning they supplement their nutrition by capturing and digesting insects. They do this because their habitat is deficient in minerals and nitrogen. Both have evolved mechanisms for capturing small prey on their glandular leaves. Once trapped by sticky hairs, bugs are dissolved by enzymes and

114

A flying insect attracted by a round-leaved sundew's flower-like leaf has been caught on the glandular hairs. Its protein will be dissolved to provide the plant with nitrogen it cannot obtain from its impoverished habitat.

absorbed. It's challenging to capture this detail on film. A good close-up will amaze friends who believe such oddities grow only in tropical jungles.

After walking around a bit you'll discover there are wetter and drier areas within the bog, and that plants tend to favour particular micro-habitats. These are localized conditions beneficial to that plant's needs. Along with the insect-digesters in wet areas are beauties such as cotton grass and tall shooting star. Even without a field guide, their descriptive names should help you identify these white and pink species.

Around the perimeter of the bog the peat moss forms hummocks. On this drier ground grow species of the heather family. Look for bog cranberry (like a miniature shooting star), Labrador tea (with fuzzy rusty underleaves), and swamp laurel (bright pink flowers). Here too survive stunted shore pines and dwarf juniper. They look like bonsai, the dwarfed potted art trees of Japan. It may have taken them several hundred years to reach this size under such difficult growing conditions.

While searching for these plants, expect to see a small frog leaping away just in front of your feet. Pacific treefrogs have sticky pads on their toes which enable them to climb shrubs and trees. For the most part they are content to clamber in the moss and low bushes. Like many land creatures on these islands, this frog has been introduced. Fortunately they have not become a problem like other non-native creatures.

Tow Hill Bog will never attract the attention of visitors like the coastal features of Naikoon Park. It does require greater effort to learn its intricacies and to appreciate its many unique and fascinating features. But none are beyond the means of anyone who is willing to spend an hour looking closely at its natural history.

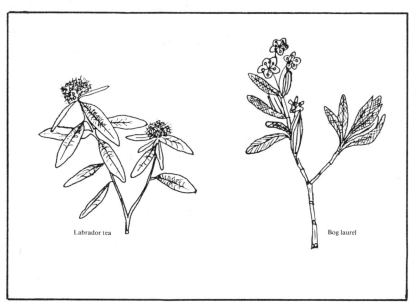

Dwarf shrubs of the bog include Labrador tea (*Ledum groenlandicum*), left and bog laurel (*Kalmia polifolia*). Labrador tea has dense clusters of white flowers, while bog laurel is intense pink. Both plants have rolled leaf edges.

16. North Beach

Getting There

North Beach stretches from the village of Haida to Rose Spit along the northeastern edge of Graham Island, and is accessible via various unmarked sideroads along its entire length. This chapter covers only the portion east of Tow Hill within Naikoon Park. A 25 km (16 mi) gravel road from Masset ends just after crossing the Hiellen River. Here vehicles can be driven directly onto the hard-packed beach sand. However, drivers unfamilar with tidal fluctuations or concerned with salt corrosion should not motor beyond this point.

North Beach is one of the most popular attractions on the Queen Charlotte Islands. Its strand is remarkably wide, firm, and beautiful. This section stretches for fifteen km (9.5 mi) from the river to the base of Rose Spit. It's a great place to enjoy the surf and sand, ride along the beach, beachcomb, or dig for clams.

The extensive beaches on the Charlottes owe their existence to glacial and water action. Sheets of ice hundreds of metres deep once slid from the Queen Charlotte Mountains carrying millions of tonnes of sand, gravel and rock. This ice melted slowly, depositing its cargo over what is now the lowlands of Graham Island and the surrounding sea.

Since the Ice Age ended, Hecate Strait and Dixon Entrance have had a dramatic effect on these glacial deposits. Nearshore currents and waves in Hecate Strait wash northward, eroding the deposits along East Beach. Similar patterns circulate fine material in Dixon Entrance. These materials move eastward towards Rose Spit. Current action, combined with onshore wind and waves, transports this sand onto the gently-sloping North Beach. In places the beach is more than two hundred m (660 ft) wide.

The temptation to drive your vehicle onto the beach is hard to resist, but a word of caution is necessary. The tide can come in with deceptive speed. Tom discovered this the hard way. As he was photographing his new truck on the beach in 1982, the incoming waves began to lick the

North Beach and Rose Spit

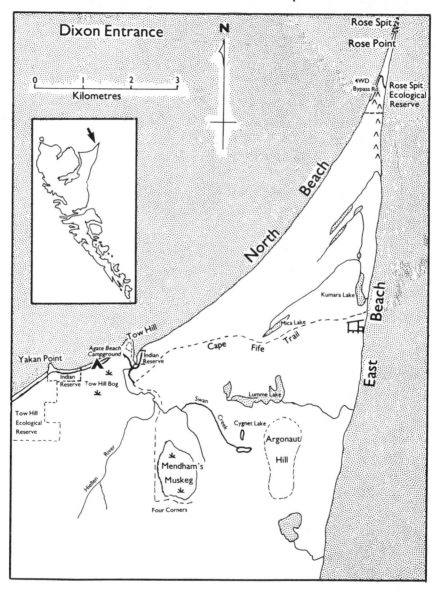

Cycling North Beach is like riding on pavement. Care needs to be taken with any vehicle taken on park beaches. Salt is a notorious corrosion agent, and loose sand at Rose Spit can grind into revolving mechanisms.

tires. Before you could say "pass the towrope," the sand softened and the vehicle settled into the beach like a nesting duck. There was no choice but to abandon the truck, head for higher ground and watch in horror as the incoming surf turned it turtle, filled the cab with sand, then flattened the vehicle into the beach.

Anyone without the aid of four-wheel drive is well advised to walk or ride a mountain bike here. We found that bicycles were by far the best way to really see the beach. They allow a round trip to the end of the beach at a leisurely pace in half a day. Please note that your bike should be thoroughly washed after a trip to prevent corrosion. There are no dependable streams along the beach, so you must clean it at the Hiellen River or the campground.

Leaving Tow Hill on a falling tide, you will have ample time to beachcomb. After every tide the beach looks different. On occasion it'll be washed completely clean. Another time you will have to navigate through every imaginable type of international flotsam. Following most storms, serious beachcombers race their competition to seize the most cherished prize — a spherical glass fishing float. These balls are break-aways from Japanese fishing nets.

Other debris includes sponges, jellyfish, shells, and even unusual

119

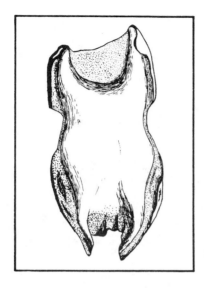

Egg case of a big skate (*Raja binoculata*) can be 22.5 cm (9 in) long. This species grows to 2.4 m (8 ft), is common over muddy bottoms, and is taken commercially.

fish. On one of Tom's trips he found a large skate. There is also a record of a great white shark being cast up on the beach. During one visit Dennis discovered a peculiar leathery pouch within a tangle of kelp. This we later identified as a mermaid's purse, which protects the embryo of a skate until the baby is strong enough to swim free.

Besides beachcombing, there are lots of other activities to occupy your time at North Beach. The shallow beach offshore makes first-class habitat for Dungeness crabs. Bright orange floats mark crab traps set by commercial boats from Masset. As the tide falls, a quick dig in the sand may expose equally delectable razor clams. In B.C. these olive-coloured shellfish occur only on this beach and Long Beach on Vancouver Island. According to fisheries officials, they seldom accumulate dangerous levels of red tide toxins which contaminate other bivalves in the Charlottes.

Razor clams are concentrated along the low tide level. They bury themselves 15 to 20 cm (6 to 8 in) beneath the sand. A shallow dimple marks their 'show'. The ideal tool for digging them is a 'clam gun', a narrow-bladed shovel. Various techniques are effective, but all require speed and care as the clams can dig quickly and fracture easily. Check the saltwater fishing regulations for bag limits.

Between 1923 and 1931 a cannery on the Hiellen River processed razor clams harvested on North Beach. After that the clams were processed in Masset, but ruins of the canning facility hidden in growth on the east bank can still be found.

Digging for razor clams (*Siliqua patula*) on North Beach. They reveal their location when you stamp on the sand. This clam can dig at 3 cm (1 in) a second. If at first you don't succeed, give up. There are plenty of others.

The experience of North Beach will be a highlight of any visit to the Queen Charlotte Islands. It's a place to walk alone when the surf is pounding and the salt spray stiffens your hair, a place to build castles of sand on sunny days, to relax around an evening campfire sharing tall tales, and to cruise along the hard sand in a dune buggy. It's hard to imagine not enjoying this special environment.

17. Rose Spit

Getting There

Rose Spit points into Dixon Entrance from the extreme northeastern corner of Graham Island. The quickest approach is via Masset, or alternately, East Beach. From Masset drive the 25 km (16 mi) gravel road to Tow Hill. From here it's a 10 km (6 mi) hike, ride, or drive along North Beach to where the trees end at the base of the spit. The land portion of the spit extends 3 km (2 mi) beyond this. Vehicles are prohibited within the ecological reserve portion of the spit.

Back at the beginning of time when the water which once covered the earth subsided, only a raven survived. In his loneliness the bird combed the islands that the broke the surface of the great sea seeking companionship. Finally, while soaring over a long sandy beach, he heard faint cries originating from a cockle shell washed up on the shore. The raven swooped down and pried the shell open. To his great wonder, the sounds grew louder and louder, and the startled bird watched in amazement as several men clambered out.

This Haida myth of human creation has been retold for centuries, and is not unlike the Christian version of worldly renewal on Mt. Ararat. The Charlottes event occurred at Nai-Kun, the long nose of Nai, which today is known as Rose Spit. The spit is held in high esteem by the natives and many visitors as one of the most interesting places throughout Haida Gwaii — the Haida homeland.

The spit has undergone several name changes over the last two hundred years. The present title gives undeserved honour to a British politician who never visited the spot. Fortunately the original name is preserved by adjacent Naikoon Provincial Park, for it's more fitting than any given by European navigators.

Rose Spit is located at the junction of North and East Beaches. Waves and currents which move along these shorelines have built an elongated neck of sand and gravel. The base is 1 km (0.6 mi) wide at the forest edge, and the spit hooks 3 km (2 mi) out to sea. An additional three km continues beneath the surface. Portions of the submarine section are visible as offshore sandbars. This is the

122

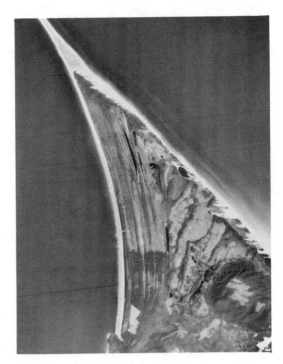

Air photo, 1973. Northward-flowing currents have extended Rose Spit several kilometres to sea. The ridges paralleling North Beach are old shorelines formed at times of higher sea levels following the last ice age.

largest such formation in the province.

The best overview of the spit is gained from atop the sand dunes at the forest edge. Prevailing winds from the southeast have shaped sand into dunes as high as 10 m (33 ft). In the process large trees have been partially buried. Many plants that grow here have thick waxy leaves or special root systems. Both represent adaptations to brutal conditions — plants are washed by salt spray, dried by the sun, pelted by drifting sand, and blown by wind. See the chapter on **Tlell Dunes** for more information on the difficult colonization of dunes by plants. From this vantage, other features of the spit are also visible.

Rose Spit is bordered on both sides by compacted driftwood. The amount of wood appears to be increasing as photos from 1960 show considerably fewer logs. In places it is possible to walk across the mass of tangled wood for 50 m (164 ft) before touching the shore.

Between the lines of logs the spit is covered by a lush meadow. Botanists have recognized three distinct plant communities which

Big-headed sedge (*Carex macrophylla*) is an important pioneer of plant colonization on dunes. It's one of the few which can establish roots in the shifting substrate.

have some interesting species. One, sea mertensia, is found nowhere else in B.C. Others such as big-head sedge and western dune tansy are found only on shòre sand. Flowering patches of yellow paintbrush and blue lupines are so fragrant that you might smell them downwind.

Plants are but one of many specialities of the spit. Upwelling currents concentrate plankton and fish near the surface, attracting many birds. Over one hundred species have been recorded here. You can expect to see shearwaters, ducks, Sandhill Cranes, and many species of gulls. During migration the area is also a mecca for shorebirds, which stop to rest and feed here. Occasionally a Peregrine Falcon will ambush the migrating peeps and plovers.

Even if birds are scarce, we highly recommend a walk to the tip of the spit. The union of Hecate Strait and Dixon Entrance creates a spectacular display. When the surf is up and the tides are changing, opposing waves smash against each other, creating a spuming liquid wall of water. Turning your back to the waves creates a most unusual sensation. The boiling sea wraps around you on three sides, leaving a narrow line of retreat. The erratic water movements have also combined to form an offshore sandbar, which is a favourite haul-out of both seals and sea lions. With binoculars, look for their large brown and gray shapes on the lee side. As an added bonus to a walk out the spit, you may be lucky enough to glimpse either gray or killer whales.

Although Rose Spit is a mecca both to wildlife and recreationists, it is a death trap to mariners. Boats have always tried to stay well out from this menacing crooked finger. Those unfortunate enough to get swept into the grasp of the vicious currents that swirl around the spit are often capsized. Over the years many lives have been lost and even some, who were lucky enough to reach the beach, died of exposure.

In 1971 all of the features of the spit were recognized under the Ecological Reserves Act by the B.C. government. The purpose of the Act is to guarantee that such places remain unaltered for scientific research. Visitors are welcome, but should be aware that camping, fires, hunting, or otherwise disturbing or removing plants and animals is illegal. Hikers and motorized vehicles are directed to stay on designated roads or beaches in this area.

Standing all alone — at the very tip of Rose Spit — is to feel like the first person on earth. One experiences what it might have been like stepping out of the clamshell after the Great Flood. The immense power of the sea before you is simultaneously humbling and rejuvenating. Behind, a whole new world. You return to it with renewed appreciation and a sense of having been touched by the spirit of Nai-Kun.

18. East Beach

Getting There

East Beach of Naikoon Park stretches continuously from the Tlell River in the south to Rose Spit on the northeast tip of Graham Island. It can be hiked starting from the north, but it is best begun at Tlell. Advice and information on current conditions may be obtained from the park headquarters located here. Before departing you may wish to self-register with the R.C.M.P. as the Parks and Outdoor Recreation Division does not keep track of backcountry users. Refer to the chapters on **Rose Spit, North Beach**, and **Tow Hill** to complete your picture of this 90 km (56 mi) hike.

At 70 km (44 mi) in length, East Beach is one of the longest in North America. A four to seven day trek along it has been steadily gaining popularity since the park was created. Though the route has no elevation change, it is still a challenge to those who enjoy backpacking. The trek offers that wonderful sense of shoreline solitude that people find so soothing to their psyche. Many hikers, familiar with more rugged terrain, have proclaimed this as a highlight in their outdoor experiences. The beach is also travelled by four-wheel drive vehicles.

The trail begins at the Tlell River bridge just north of Misty Meadows Campground. From the picnic site at the bridge, a 2 km (1.2 mi) trail parallels the north side of the river through the forest, to the beach. A faster alternate is to follow Beitush Road along the river's south bank, then wade the river at low tide. It's only knee-deep at a stony ford. By walking northward from this point, you keep the prevailing wind, rain, and sun out of your eyes.

Before heading out on this adventure you are well advised to prepare for all kinds of weather conditions as even in summer there can be fog and cool temperatures. It's also essential to carry a watch and valid tide table. You'll need these to time your crossing of unbridged tidal rivers. Caution! This is basically an unpatrolled wildland and parties in trouble cannot be rescued by sea.

From the mouth of the Tlell River the beach is beautiful. To

Wreck of the barge *Pesuta*. Built about 1919, she was under tow when a gale blew the tug near the shallows, which extend far out from this shore. *Pesuta* went aground and was abandoned after the tow line snapped.

seaward, an unbroken but ever-changing expanse of cloud and wave stetches from horizon to horizon. In the foreground, Semipalmated Plovers scurry down the long beach which fades to infinity. On the left stretches a continuous line of sand cliffs or dunes, topped by spruce forest. A few days of such spectacular scenic monotony satisfies some; others take ten delightful days to reach the end of this magnificent trip.

Four kilometres (2.5 mi) from the picnic site is the bow remnant of the 1928 shipwreck *Pesuta*. This wooden barge was under tow in Hecate Strait when its line parted in a winter storm. The barge and its cargo of logs became driftwood. When looking at the millions of drift logs on these islands, note how few are of natural origin (i.e. unsawn). Virtually all have been lost from log booms over the past five or six decades. Driftwood, at least on the Charlottes, is largely a man-made phenomenon.

A couple of hours walk north of the wreck brings you to Cape Ball River, a good overnight location. Please respect the private property here, and pitch tents near the park hiking shelter. Private holdings such as lots 1357 and 1358 still exist within the park, and are noted on topographic maps of 1:50,000 scale.

The tide floods the mouth of this river, as well as the others along this route. Fresh water and a crossing can only be gained during low tide. A receding tide is also necessary to pass the 60 m (200 ft) sand

Hiking around the cliffs at Cape Ball. The layers of sand were laid down by a dirty river flowing from melting glaciers into the sea. The occasional boulder between the layers was dropped from a drifting ice floe.

cliffs at Cape Ball. The trek around this headland north to Eagle Hill may take as long as five hours. Eagle Creek is the only break in this wall which allows a retreat from incoming waves.

Recently some very exciting research has been done on these cliffs and on the plain beyond. The implications of the discoveries are altering our perception of geologic events in British Columbia. Consequently, other fields of research are reforming their theories on the biological, climatic, and cultural history of the Charlottes.

This site was chosen for investigation because the uncompressed sediments were deposited in chronological order during and after the Ice Age. Researchers have determined that melting of the provincial ice cap throughout most of B.C. began about 10,000 years ago. However, geologist John Clague of the Geological Survey of Canada and biologist Rolf Mathewes of Simon Fraser University have discovered plant remains in these cliffs dating 16,000 years before the present.

There were actually trees and peat bogs here when continental Canada was as stiff as an icicle! This evidence strengthens the possibility that there was an 'oasis' or refugium during the last big chill. If all these features were in place, could there have been animals or people present? Stay tuned to the Charlottes as the edge

128

East Beach of Naikoon Park facing Hecate Strait. This view looks south past Kumara Lake. There is good camping in this vicinity.

of science probes these possibilities.

Moving north along the beach, there are nice camping spots at Eagle Creek, Lot 114 A (where there is another shelter), the Oeanda River mouth, and Kumara Lake. The availability of fresh water determines where you camp each night. Rivers are either tidal, of periodic flow, or enter the ocean beneath the beach, making it difficult to obtain drinking water. Topographic maps will help you locate streams on this featureless coast.

In a pinch water can be taken from ponds in the interior. All surface water in the park is tea-coloured, having been drained through peat. The Scots may claim it makes better whiskey, but we advise boiling or otherwise purifying it before drinking. Flavoured juice crystals make the taste more palatable. Alternatively, a plastic tarp serves as both a cooking shelter and water-catcher. It will funnel rain into a water bottle when used as a flysheet or when laid across a sandy depression overnight.

Nearing Kumara Lake sand dunes become prominent. Look for places where sand-buried trees have been uncovered by high waves of recent storms. In other areas, you can find marine shells embedded in mud banks above the present sea level. Obviously this land has not always been the way it appears today. This landscape is in transformation.

Dune formation and erosion are natural processes, but they are accelerated by the removal of stabilizing plants (see **Tlell River and**

Sand Dunes chapter). Regrettably, in places around Rose Spit, plants and their supporting dunes have been damaged by 4-wheeling trucks. According to the park master plan of 1983, these infernal-combustion machines are supposed to be prohibited from this wild beach. For a time they were, but partisan politicians reversed this decision under local pressure.

There is another hiking shelter at Cape Fife, where a trail leads past the southern end of Kumara Lake directly to Tow Hill. This inland route cuts 10 km off completion of your trek via North Beach. But since you would miss beautiful Rose Spit to the north, we recommend the trail option only if time is short. Hikers exiting via Cape Fife will have to visit the spit on a subsequent day or be forever sorry.

Topographic Maps

These topographic maps cover the entire hike, and may be purchased at the Government Agent Office in Queen Charlotte City or mail-ordered from:

Map and Air Photo Sales
Surveys and Resource Mapping Branch
Ministry of Crown Lands
Parliament Buildings
Victoria, B.C.
V8V lX5

Map Sales Office
Geological Survey of Canada
100 West Pender Street
Vancouver, B.C. V6B lR8

NTS 1:50,000 scale

103 G/12 West Tlell
103 G/13 West Eagle Hill
103 G/13 East Eagle Hill
103 J/4 West Tow Hill
103 J/4 East Tow Hill

Tide tables relevant to the Queen Charlottes are *Volume 6, Barkley Sound and Discovery Passage to Dixon Entrance*. See Chapter 1, **Navigation** for where to order.

19. Tlell River and Sand Dunes

Getting There

Tlell is an unincorporated hamlet scattered around the southern edge of Naikoon Park. Here Yellowhead Highway No. 16 crosses the Tlell River on a wooden bridge. It is located 42 km (26 mi) north of the Skidegate Landing ferry dock and 21 km (13 mi) south of Port Clements. Within 1 km (0.5 mi) south of the river are the park headquarters and Misty Meadows Campground.

The Tlell area has the most extensive sand dunes in British Columbia. This location provides a great opportunity to walk among them. The river is also known internationally for its salmon fishing. This chapter is divided between two walks which explore these attractions. Carry this guide along to identify features en route.

Sand Dunes

Before heading to the dunes, check the information shelter outside park headquarters. An interpretive plaque here shows flowers you can expect to see later. The shelter also details local facilities and services. The nearest campground is Misty Meadows, only half a kilometre down the road. This park facility has thirty sites, pit toilets, and a tap for drinking water. The campground is serviced daily, is open year-round, and a fee is charged May through September. Even though it can fill quickly, reservations are not accepted.

A return walk to see the dunes begins from the campground and can be comfortably completed in two hours. Start on the trail at the parking/picnic area which leads to the beach. Once through the trees, take note of some landmarks as many people miss the exit from the beach on their return. Head south, or to your right, and follow the forest edge along the coast. Within fifteen minutes you'll come to the first dunes.

Is the wind on your left cheek? Probably so, because the prevailing wind direction is from the southeast. Sou'easterlies are the most frequent and the strongest winds in the Charlottes. Without them there would be no dunes.

131

Tlell River and Sand Dunes

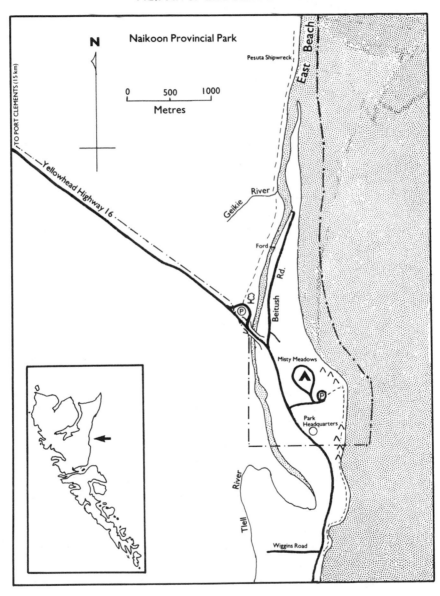

Along this coast of Graham Island massive sand deposits are being eroded and deposited onto the beaches. Where the ground behind the beach is low-lying, wind-blown sand forms dunes. These moving mounds often reach impressive size. Active dunes are sparsely vegetated.

When you arrive where the dunes are advancing, note the parallel zones which characterize this area. At the front is the surf zone. Its limit is defined by fresh drift logs. Behind them is a narrow zone of older driftwood, often partially buried. Behind that is a transition zone. This is an ecological no-man's land where sand dunes and plantlife fight one another for supremacy. The final zone is the fringing forest. This is the plants' ultimate defense in stopping the dunes' activity.

Take a careful walk across these zones and you'll see how strong the force is that moves this sand. On the windward side of old fenceposts, the grain has been raised by the blasting and chiseling action of wind-blown sand. In the transition zone you might find a ventifact. This is a stone with glossy surfaces and sharp ridges which the wind has sand-blasted. Finally, on the dunes you will see dead trees. The large branches protruding from the trunk at ground level show that some have been smothered by sand to depths of 10 m (33 ft).

These dunes actually start at the driftwood. Sand is picked up here by wind and moved until it meets an obstruction. Thus small dunes accumulate around rocks, driftwood, or even plants. As the dune grows in size it acts as a windbreak. The sand rolls up the windward slope, then drops over the lee side. By tiny granular increments the size of the dune grows and it is pushed before the wind. Small dunes travel faster than large ones, so they ultimately merge with others. Note that the landscape features here are all aligned in the direction of the prevailing wind.

As dunes travel across the transition zone, plants attempt to cover them. Grasses and sedges are particularly suited for this type of action. As sand piles around their stems, they send up new leaf shoots. They can grow rhizomes (horizontal subterranean stems) very quickly, and green leaves pop up all along this system. This method of rapid reproduction is much more effective than the annual setting of seeds in this shifting environment. Here you might recognize species such as bighead sedge or wild strawberry.

These plants are pioneers, trying to stabilize the dune with their rhizomes and runners. If they succeed, other plants like dune tansy

This massive blow-out in a dune has eroded right down to a former beach. Such erosion is very difficult to stop, and the sand can move on to bury good pastureland or forest. Note the alignment of landforms in this area.

and beach lupine can get a start. If they fail, the wind may resume the dune's progress. Or a blowout may occur. This is an erosional hollow blown out of a disturbed dune. This happens when root systems are damaged by drought, grazing cattle, beach buggies, or trampling by people. Each plant is important. Walk carefully — avoid crushing plants or making a rut.

Generally, dunes at the forest edge are fully vegetated. The trees prevent further progress. On the forest side of these dunes, mosses and shrubs have formed a stable plant community. At the southern-most end of the walk, note how grass has successfully covered the dunes.

About an hour after starting you will see hydro-electric poles above the beach. From here you may choose to return along the highway to see the dunes from their lee side. The distance is about the same as the way you have come.

Tlell River

The second walk from the campground takes you in the opposite direction. If you're an angler, you probably headed this way first — never mind the sand dunes! The Tlell River bridge is just a short walk along the highway north of the campground. The river has good access along its lower reaches since Beitush Road parallels the south bank. Many people concentrate in the section downstream of the bridge because they get to cast first at fish coming in with flood tides.

The main species of interest here is coho salmon which run from the first week of September to mid-October. The timing will be dependent on the fall rains; the fish hold offshore until river levels are high enough for successful spawning. Their peak is midway between these times with fish averaging 5.6 kg (12 lbs), with a maximum of 9 kg (20 lbs). Green Krocodile lures are favoured.

The Tlell also is known for steelhead, although this run isn't as good as it used to be. These sea-going trout reach weights of 4.6 kg (10 lbs) and enter the river from early February through April. Fishing is on both the upper and lower sections.

If you miss these runs, take heart, as the Tlell also has good cutthroat trout fishing in the spring and early summer. These fish go to sea and are caught on their return. Dolly Varden up to 2 kg (4 lbs) can also be caught in mid-summer. Be certain to check the tidal and non-tidal fishing regulations as they change from year to year. Fishing licences are not sold by park staff. The nearest place tackle and licences can be obtained is Port Clements.

If you have time, walk along either bank toward the river mouth. Note how the river is bent north, paralleling the beach. Currents flow north in such a way that a small spit has been extended here in the same fashion as the one at Rose Spit. The wreck of the *Pesuta* is visible from a long distance (see preceding chapter). If you return to the campground via the beach, allow three hours for the round trip.

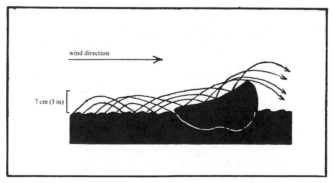

The flattened face of a ventifact is cut by the impact of wind-driven sand grains. The stone's surface has a characteristic sheen and a distinct ridge.

20. Gray Bay

Getting There

The 4 km (2.5 mi) crescent beach at Gray Bay is located south of Sandspit on the northeast side of Moresby Island. From Sandspit, Copper Bay Road will lead you to Gray Bay within an hour. This road is poorly signed, so watch for it at 13.1 km (8.2 mi) from the Alliford Bay ferry dock. This partially-paved road heads south, passing the airport and numerous shacks at Copper Bay. At 19 km (11.9 mi) a distinct left fork, Spur 20, leads east for an additional 9 km (5.6 mi) to Gray Bay. A longer alternate route from Alliford Bay will also bring you here, but you need to recognize the turn-off from the opposite direction.

Portions of these private roads are open to the public. Fletcher Challenge Canada hauls logs in different locations at unscheduled intervals. During working hours on weekdays, visitors must stop at their office in Sandspit for information on current logging activity:

Fletcher Challenge Canada
453 Beach Road
Sandspit, B.C. V0T 1T0
Telephone: (604) 637-5436

Note: The campsite at Gray Bay lacks clear drinking water, so fill water containers before arriving.

After turning from Copper Bay Road, alders and hemlock overhang the bumpy, one-lane Spur 20. A small bridge crossing Gray Bay Creek marks your entry to Gray Bay and a B.C. Forest Service recreation site. Twelve separated campsites have been cleared along the road paralleling the beach. All the sites have tables and nearby pit toilets, but only two have kitchen shelters. No fee is charged. Within a few paces of each site is one of the best beaches on the islands. Soft gray sand arcs around a gentle bay reminiscent of a tropical paradise. Low tide exposes sand flats stretching well out from shore. Throw off your shoes and tantalize your toes in the bubbling surf.

When you're ready to explore beyond the beach, a sign at Gray Bay

Gray Bay to Cumshewa Head

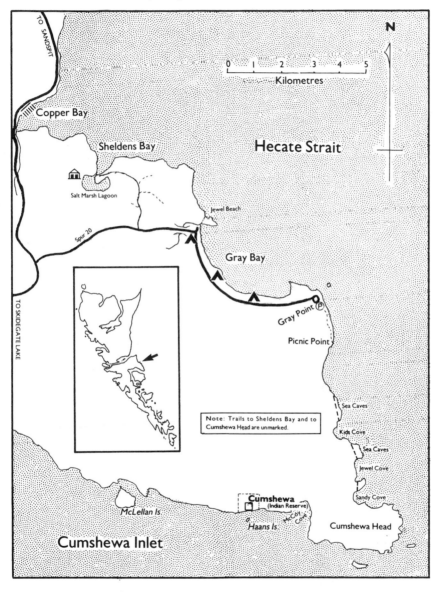

TO SANDSPIT

Copper Bay

Sheldens Bay

Salt Marsh Lagoon

Spur 20

TO SKIDEGATE LAKE

Hecate Strait

N

0 1 2 3 4 5
Kilometres

Jewel Beach

Gray Bay

Gray Point

Picnic Point

Sea Caves

Kids Cove

Sea Caves

Jewel Cove

Sandy Cove

Note: Trails to Sheldens Bay and to
Cumshewa Head are unmarked.

McLellan Is.

Cumshewa
(Indian Reserve)

Haans Is.

McCoy Cove

Cumshewa Head

Cumshewa Inlet

Creek shows nearby hiking opportunities. The shortest trail begins at the mouth of Gray Bay Creek. Wade across the shallows at low tide. On the opposite bank, a five-minute walk through the trees ends at Jewel Beach. In this secluded spot your cares can recede to sea with the tide. Soaring eagles will transport your mind to tranquil memories.

You'll need more time to walk or bicycle along the road paralleling Gray Bay. Each campsite allows access to different sections of the beach. The road south ends in a clearing with a cement foundation. These remains are an old LORAN (Long Range Navigation) station. LORAN electronics, now located at Williams Lake in the interior of B.C., allow planes and ships to determine their latitude and longitude extremely accurately.

Trails lead from here to Gray Point and south to Cumshewa Head. The trip to Cumshewa Head and back involves a full-day hike. For the first portion, a minimal trail parallels the beach. Families with small children could walk along this section, reaching a picnic spot in under an hour. Beyond that point the trail deteriorates into a poorly-marked route along beaches, deer trails, and awkward rocky scrambles.

Keen hikers may wish to tackle this trail during the long days of summer when this latitude experiences seventeen hours of light at the solstice. A round trip to the head takes twelve to fourteen hours. Plan to leave Gray Point just after a high tide to avoid being caught by water. Sea caves, rocky outcrops, and tidepools are the attractions. Also watch for seals and river otters in the surf. Take a marine chart and topographic map to track your progress, as well as plenty of snacks and drinking water. This is one of the few hikes mentioned in this book where hiking boots have a definite advantage over gum boots.

If Cumshewa Head is beyond your means, try hiking to Sheldens Bay. The easiest route to it begins 5 km (3.1 mi) back along the road from the bridge at Gray Bay Creek. An inactive logging road branches right into a clear-cut. This spur forks frequently, but with a topographic map and some persistence, you'll find the bay with a salt marsh behind it. Few people go here, so it's a nice spot to wander about for an afternoon. Several homesteaders lived here in the early 1900's, but little remains of their dwellings. Now the lagoon is a haven for deer and migrating waterfowl. Look for dabbling ducks, shorebirds, and Great Blue Herons. You may be lucky enough to spot Trumpeter Swans or Sandhill Cranes.

Flooding sea cave on the coastal hike between Gray Point and Cumshewa Head. This rugged 10 km (6 mi) walk is recommended only for fit scramblers.

Gray Bay is typical of the Charlottes, as many attractive qualities of the islands are found here. Sandy beaches are sheltered by rough volcanic headlands. Scattered beneath giant spruce and hemlock, the rustic campsites ensure privacy, yet link to nearby roads and trails. Several days of relaxing, walking, wave-watching, or birding will easily fill your time. You'll find Gray Bay a nice introduction to the Charlottes.

21. Pallant Creek Fish Hatchery

Getting There

Pallant Creek is located approximately 48 km (30 mi) south of Sandspit. It's reached by travelling through Sandspit and past the Gray Bay turn-off, or by turning right immediately after disembarking the ferry at Alliford Bay. Both these gravel roads are in good condition as they are used by logging companies. They eventually join at a well-marked turn-off. This branch leads past Pallant Creek hatchery to Moresby Camp. Allow an hour for driving here from the ferry or Sandspit.

Before leaving for the hatchery, it's advisable to phone 637-5436, the Fletcher Challenge Canada office for details on logging traffic. They provide maps from their office at 453 Beach Road in Sandspit.

For more information contact:
Dept. of Fisheries and Oceans
Box 208
Queen Charlotte City, B.C. VOT 1SO
Telephone: (604) 559-4754

Fishing has always been important to the islands' economy. Salmon and trout were once so numerous they were believed to be inexhaustible. Poor logging practices and over-fishing have combined to seriously deplete fish stocks in recent decades. This prompted the construction of a hatchery on Pallant Creek which flows into Cumshewa Inlet on Moresby Island. Operated by the Federal Department of Fisheries and Oceans, this is a prime example of conservation in action.

This Japanese-style facility was designed primarily to raise chum, the most abundant salmon spawning on these islands. In late August and September, adults returning to spawn are held back by a 'fence' across the creek. For several weeks, Fisheries staff dip-net the adults and transfer them to holding ponds where they remain until 'ripe'. Their brilliant silver sides turn a dull green with purple blotches. This signals that the fish are ready to spawn.

Then technicians artificially strip each female of her 2400 eggs and

Skidegate Inlet

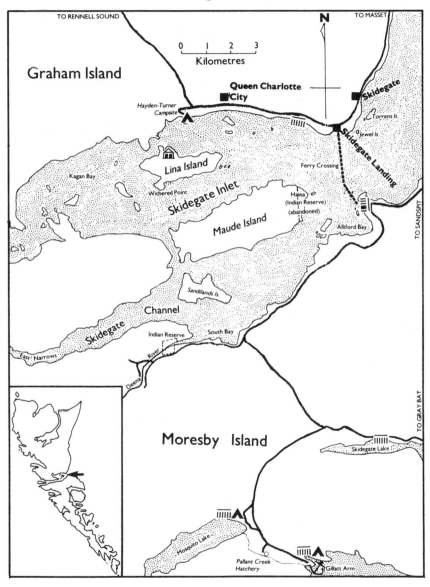

Fertilized eggs in a Heath tray. Fresh water percolates through successive trays, carrying oxygen in and metabolic by-products out. Hatching time varies with water temperature (approximately 50 days in water at 10°C).

stroke the males to release creamy milt, or sperm. Fertilization takes place, and up to 100,000 eggs are placed in a single Atkins box. Others are incubated in Heath trays which hold only 7000 eggs. Both containers allow creek water to circulate through them. Moving water brings oxygen to developing embryos and deters fungal growth.

During the next sixty days the eggs pass through an 'eyed' stage, then hatch as alevins. Alevins are tiny fish with a yolk sac attached to their belly. The sac functions as a lunch bucket supplying the developing fish with nourishment. It slowly shrinks as the food is absorbed. You can only witness this at a hatchery since these stages normally occur beneath the gravel in a creek. Once the sac is depleted, the young fish, or fry, are free-swimming voracious appetites. In the wild they wiggle from the gravel and head for the ocean where there is abundant food. These hatchery fry are penned at the ocean's edge, where they gobble enriched food for speedy growth.

An interesting problem occurred at these pens in Gillatt Arm. Predatory rockfish and perch outside the pens ate large numbers of fry within a few hours of their release. After unsuccessful attempts to solve the problem, fishery technicians decided to tow the pens 20 km (12.6 mi) down Cumshewa Inlet. They believed if the released fish can easily escape, more will return to spawn. The results of this experiment will be known when the first three-year olds return in 1988. Since the hatchery releases about ten million fry annually, even a small increase in survival will be noticeable.

In 1987 renovations at Pallant Creek increased the hatchery's capacity by more than five million fish. These additional fry are released in Mathers Creek on nearby Louise Island. Most are chum, but about 400,000 coho are also let go. The coho will be a boon to the sport fishery. From late August through September of 1988, 3000 coho were caught as they returned through Cumshewa Inlet. These numbers will improve as hatchery capacity increases. Pallant Creek also has a wild steelhead run in the winter and spring months.

This hatchery is part of the Salmonid Enhancement Program (SEP). Despite some criticism, its goal of increasing both fish stocks and public awareness in British Columbia is working. SEP has been aided by another equally important program known as the Public Involvement Program, or PIP. This program involves school and service groups, and many interested individuals, who have volunteered time clearing streams, monitoring incubators, or assisting fisheries officials. PIP and SEP, now in their tenth year, are success stories.

However, some of the problems which initially gave rise to the Pallant Creek Hatchery remain unsolved. This became obvious in the fall of 1979 when a series of storms dumped copious amounts of rainfall on the islands. As a result an unusual number of landslides destroyed several important salmon streams. Public outrage resulted. Logging companies were accused of logging slopes too steep to tolerate clear-cuts, and of poor roadbuilding techniques which triggered the slides. Angry exchanges took place locally and in the provincial legislature. A five year study program, with a mandate to determine the causes of slides, investigate rehabilitation programs, and assess tree planting and logging methods was initiated.

The results of these studies do not paint a favourable picture as far as our logging industry is concerned. Recent revelations show that there are six times as many landslides on logged sites as on natural sites. Studies also show that the present rate of harvest exceeds the rate of forest regeneration, that up to twenty percent of potentially useable wood is left as debris on logged sites, and that logged areas are not adequately replanted. All these horrors continue to damage spawning habitat, particularly on Graham Island.

Only adequate forest regeneration will completely solve the fish/forestry problems. There is a bit of good news, however. In 1988 a $24 million Forest Replacement Fund was established by the federal and provincial governments as part of the South Moresby National Park Reserve agreement. The money will be spent over the next eight years to increase the growth potential of the forests outside the park boundaries.

Despite earlier setbacks, Pallant Creek continues to strengthen its fish stocks. Fry are fed daily during April and May. Visitors are welcome to view this and other activites, but must book in advance. If you're travelling to Cumshewa Inlet, plan to view the largest hatchery on the islands.

22. Louise Island Circumnavigation

Getting There

Louise Island and Cumshewa Inlet are in the North Moresby region, and are accessible by boat and helicopter, though floatplanes also land at two logging camps. Trailered boats are best launched at Moresby Camp, a former logging encampment on Gillatt Arm of Cumshewa Inlet, which can be reached by gravel roads leading from the ferry dock at Alliford Bay on Skidegate Inlet or from Sandspit. The route is marked, but may have log-hauling activity on portions of it. Check with Fletcher Challenge Canada (637-5436) in Sandspit before driving. Shuttle service for kayakers without a vehicle is available in Sandspit, but people with plenty of time and energy have paddled into this area right from the ferry dock at Skidegate Landing.

Louise Island is the third-largest island in the Charlottes. If your time or inclination is limited, the circuit around it provides a taste of the wild archipelago further south. Louise Island has ancient archaeology, recent relics, natural history, and the opportunity to see the Moresby region from its maritime aspect. This tandem chapter is divided to accomodate those who wish to complete only the Moresby Camp to Skedans portion.

For anyone wanting to spend several days fishing and camping in the inlet, a B.C. Forest Service recreation site in the trees at Moresby Camp provides rudimentary facilities. A similar campsite with 11 spaces and a picnic shelter has been built at nearby Mosquito Lake. No fees are collected at either location. The Canadian Parks Service plans to start construction of a proper boat ramp, campground, and information centre in Gordon Cove as early as 1989.

Waterways around Louise Island are generally protected, but some open directly onto Hecate Strait. Cartop boaters and canoeists do venture out that far, though they need to beware the wind. Such exposed waters can be rough, and on one occasion we waited five hours for a northeaster to calm enough to allow us to round Skedans Point. Our inflatable made the trip successfully, but as we passed we

Sandspit to Louise Island

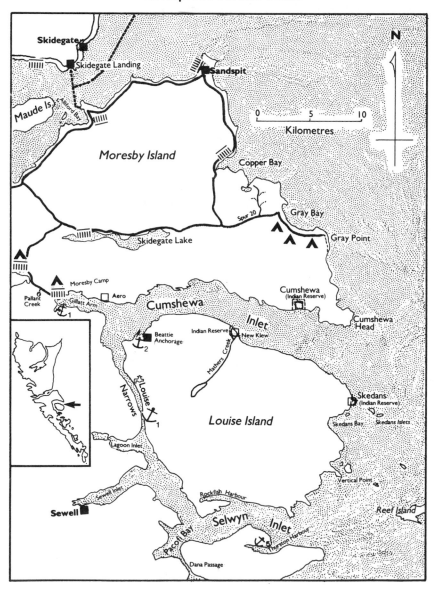

couldn't help but notice a double kayak drawn up on a boulder-strewn beach with everything laid out to dry.

Cumshewa Inlet sees a lot of traffic as there's a logging camp at Beattie Anchorage on the northwest coast of Louise Island, and another in Sewell Inlet which uses Carmichael Passage for access. Yachters will appreciate the five mooring buoys in Thurston Harbour on Talunkwan Island and another two at Beattie Anchorage. There is one in Gordon Cove. Craft heading south from here can fill with fresh water in Carmichael Passage just north of Louise Narrows. A sign indicates the plastic pipe on a log float.

Cumshewa Inlet

Cumshewa Inlet is a deep marine indentation with Moresby Camp at its head being the launch point for boaters heading to southern islands and passages. In 1988 the marine 'facilities' were a dilapidated float, single mooring buoy, and a gravel beach for trailered boat launching. This beach is not suitable for underpowered vehicles or the launching of heavy boats. More than one visitor whose equipment didn't measure up has found himself stuck on the beach. From here Cumshewa Inlet can be explored by motor boat in one day.

Logging is still active on the south shore of the inlet, and some visitors find the clear-cuts a detracting eyesore. And it's very hard to argue with that sentiment. Still, those of us who use paper and live in timber buildings must consider our opinions carefully. Moresby Island residents are understandably touchy about criticism of their livelihood. Logging has gone on here for decades, and most cut areas are regenerating nicely. We've walked in forests which initially looked virgin, but were surprised to find stumps. Mother nature knows her business!

During World War II up to ten logging camps existed on this inlet. Crews bundled logs into heavy rafts called Davis rafts for towing south to mainland mills at a speed of two or three knots. There was enough wood in some rafts to cut over two million board feet of lumber. (A board foot is a plank measuring one inch thick by one foot square.) Such wooden icebergs were expensive to move, but saved the high log losses associated with unbundled booms. Today's self-loading, self-dumping, self-propelled log barges are the most interesting vessels plying these inlets.

The biggest logging operation in this area was Aero, named for

These self-loading barges remove logs to mills on B.C.'s lower mainland. They slide their loads off by flooding tanks on one side of the vessel. No sawmill in the Charlottes has ever shipped lumber off-island.

the airplane (Sitka) spruce. Aero had the only logging railroad on the Charlottes, and track ran from the ocean over the hill to Skidegate Lake. Steep hills required the use of geared-drive locomotives which sounded like they were going ninety, but actually crawled up the steep grades with massive loads — sometimes only one log to a car. In the bush at Aero are the remains of several such flatcars and a locomotive. Their old roadbeds have grown up with emerald grass to form cultivated paths through tunnels of second-growth alders. Spikes of flowered foxglove and lupine are healing the embankments, but the feeling here is peculiar. Today it's hard to imagine the steaming shriek of the locos and the roar of the two-man chainsaws used here in 1945.

Invisible from the water is a monstrous fuel storage tank which rises to the height of the forest canopy. Finding it standing within this forest is like discovering a piece of civilization out of context. We were reminded of the technological monolith raised in the Amazon jungle by the eccentric inventor in Paul Theroux's book *The Mosquito Coast*. Aero is one of the more interesting abandoned European sites to explore in the Charlottes as its ruins are widely distributed, not extensively overgrown, and are easily accessible.

Across the inlet and further east is more logging activity at Mathers Creek, also called Church Creek for the place of worship which once stood here. This watershed was first cut during the war years as well, but hauling here was done on ingenious log roads. Trucks with hard rubber tires ran on flattened log 'rails'. A number of these vehicles remain in the second-growth a few minutes' walk west of the creek. Unfortunately the lack of light and dense tree trunks make them a challenge to photograph. Old machinery also lays within the tidal zone, so boaters should use caution to avoid hull punctures.

Mathers Creek is also the location of the former village of New Kloo (also spelled Clew). This short-lived native settlement was built in 1887 in contemporary style. People came here from Tanu (Kloo) after that village deteriorated from contact with a European culture counter to their own. Reverend Thomas Crosby helped build the new town, including a plant for the extraction of oil from dogfish livers. The oil was sold for lubricating machinery and lighting lamps.

Despite the brave effort, New Kloo was abandoned in 1897 in favour of more-worldly Skidegate. The concentration of community facilities at the latter location made it sensible for scattered villages to amalgamate. The experience humiliated the survivors of Tanu. Only twenty years earlier their original village held 547 people — one of the largest populations in this archipelago. Their headstones along Mathers Creek bear many familiar surnames — Clew, Ninstence, and Capt. Skdance. In recent years some of these graves have been robbed, an unforgiveable desecration.

Moving down the inlet toward Hecate Strait, don't be surprised if you encounter small groups of porpoises. Of the two species common in the Charlottes, harbour porpoises are most likely found within such a fjord. They are shy and will not tolerate pursuit. Be on the look-out for their gray backs and triangular dorsal fins disappearing into the distance. Occasionally porpoises are caught in the gillnets of commercial fishermen who take advantage of the enhanced stocks of salmon returning to spawn in Pallant and Mathers creeks.

Cumshewa Inlet and Gillatt Arm are popular with sport fishermen who come between mid-August and September to angle for coho salmon. Several ships have anchored here as floating lodges for well-heeled clients. They troll herring as a very effective bait, but the locals like green Buzz Bombs and pink hoochies. Try your luck!

Good fishing is almost assured in these waters because the salmon are concentrated as they pass up the narrow inlet. The steep sides and plunging depths of this marine valley are characteristic of routes once gouged by glaciers. All of British Columbia's coast has these fjords,

Upright timbers at the former village of Cumshewa. These cedar planks likely flanked a central totem at the gable end of a house. Haida buildings were not longhouses, a term for dissimilar structures of the south coast.

which were enlarged during the last Ice Age. B.C. geologist A. Sutherland Brown has found evidence that this location was covered by a thousand metres of ice. This frozen flow was generated in the mountains to the west and ground slowly toward Hecate Strait. You might imagine it as Mother Earth's mover, scraping soil from the hills and pushing a ridge of rubble before it. When the ice melted, it left a mound across the mouth of this inlet. Marine charts label this as Fairburn Shoals, and it marks a terminus of the former icefront.

Fairburn Shoals are covered by a huge bed of bull kelp which forms a significant navigation problem, especially at low tide. When the tide is high, you might find a narrow clear passage along the shoreline. This route saved our skins one day when a heavy swell topped by whitecaps made the inlet dangerous. Sneaking our inflatable in the lee of the kelp, we found the water much smoother.

Near here is the village which is the namesake for the inlet. Very little remains at Cumshewa. Several totems and some leaning house planks have been nearly defeated by growing trees. At low tide you can walk out to Haans Islet, a former burial site in front of the village. Although infrequently visited, Cunshewa has a pleasant, serene atmosphere.

Skedans on Louise Island is probably the most popular abandoned village on the Charlottes. In 1878 the famous Canadian geologist George Dawson photographed fifty-six totems standing here before a row of twenty-seven houses. A more recent book, *Those Born at Koona*, by John and Carloyn Smyly describes these totems in detail, and is a useful on-site guide.

Several books have been written about abandoned Haida villages. They are useful in the field to identify totems and understand the complex society that erected them. Children's books on the subject are also available.

Sadly, most of the totems here have succumbed to the pull of gravity. We've noted visible deterioration in those still standing even over the past few years. Such decay is inevitable, but still we wish we'd been able to visit here with painter Emily Carr in 1912. This was before the superior totems rotted or were collected by museums. Today one remarkable specimen is nearly indistinguishable from a rotting log. On the pathside at the western edge of the village is the carved figure of a wolf. It crouches horizontally as a memorial to some deceased authority. A large tree now grows from its back, and moss obscures the figure's minor defining lines. When you suddenly recognize its form, the surprise is not unlike being startled by a live beast in the grass.

More than a century has passed since this carving was released from bondage in a cedar log. Now it's returning to the earth which claimed its carver and his village. This wolf's supernatural ability to snap our vision is not unlike the Haida belief in transformations. It demonstrates the power in native art and is indicative of Haida kinship with nature.

Skedans through Louise Narrows

Lying 7 km out in Hecate Strait are the Skedans Islands and Reef Island. The far side of these islands are frequented by Steller sea lions. Up to one hundred of these animals might be seen here, though their numbers have declined despite being protected since 1970 under the Federal Fisheries Act. Ancient Haida were known to kill these marine behemoths, and the figures of sea lions appeared

151

Rusting boilers in Pacofi Bay are breaking down rapidly in the saltchuck. Few of the many packing operations attempted here over a 40-year period were financially successful. Most fish plants are now urbanized.

on totems which once stood in the village of Skedans.

The natives also once had a small village at Vertical Point, but no evidence can be seen of it today. In wet weather paddlers will be pleased to find a tiny cabin here where a New York artist painted in recent summers. Vertical takes its name from upturned limestone beds at the point. Beaches on either side provide safe landings in northerly or southerly winds. Another cabin is at nearby Skedans Creek, where water is assured. Both are good camping sites when planning a visit to Skedans, since overnight stays are prohibited within that Indian reserve.

We have found some industrial settlements as interesting as abandoned Haida villages. Like the native villages, these too are fast disappearing beneath the encroaching rainforest. In the next millenium archeologists may be unearthing places such as Pacofi to reveal clues as to why the white, Japanese, and native men worked in the same building but resided in separate quarters.

Pacofi is an acronym of the Pacific Coast Fisheries plant which began operation in 1910 in the bay of the same name. Many rusty remnants are still visible here. Over the years a packing plant, a saltery, an oil and fertilizer reduction plant, and a plant for making potash from kelp operated periodically. B.C. Packers demolished most of the buildings in 1949, but machinery still remains in the woods and on the beach. Use caution when landing your boat as there are submerged concrete blocks and metal all along this shore.

An evening may be passed quietly in Rockfish Harbour on the southwest corner of Louise Island. Its name didn't fulfill our angling expectations, but this bay does have protected anchorage and fresh water for campers. Regretably, we hear that Rockfish is proposed for a logging camp.

In nearby Sewell Inlet there is presently such a camp, actually a small company town of Western Forest Products Ltd. About one hundred loggers and their families live here, half the number there used to be. Residents blame this decline on formation of the national park. Their pub is called the Full Boar Inn. Dennis was tempted to go in and meet some of the locals, but reconsidered after speaking with Dave the trucker: "I wouldn't want to be an environmentalist in there on Friday night. That's what you call livin' dangerously."

If this talk of bottled fluid and suds makes you thirsty, you might want to visit Lagoon Inlet. Here a bedrock bottleneck retards tidal movement in and out of a shallow basin. Levels between the inlet and lagoon may vary by a metre, creating lots of froth as the water races to catch up. River otters often play in this reversing rapid, and deer and bear graze along the estuary. Camping is good inside the 'bottle', but plan your departure so you're not left dry as the jellyfish when the contents are drained.

Returning to Moresby Camp, Louise Narrows is a dredged channel, providing high tide slack passage between Louise and Moresby islands for large motor vessels. Moving through during tidal changes is similar to running a river, and paddlers won't be able to make progress 'upstream'. Prior to its excavation in 1967, this location resembled Burnaby Narrows because the flushing action draws abundant nutrients for marine organisms. Life in the shallows at the south end of Louise Narrows indicates the intertidal array to be found at the latter locale.

For information on forest recreation and management on Moresby Island south of Mosquito Lake, contact:
Resident Forester
Western Forest Products Ltd.
Sewell Inlet, B.C. V0T 1V0
Telephone: (604) 637-2201
There are emergency services only in Sewell Inlet and the logging camp at Beattie Anchorage.

Introduction to South Moresby National Park Reserve

During the early 1970s the Canadian government became interested in the South Moresby region as a potential site for a national park. However, it was only after international attention was focused on the proposal that enough political will was created to preserve the area's scenic, recreational, biological, and cultural phenomena. On July 11, 1987 the federal government in Ottawa and the provincial government in Victoria signed a memorandum of agreement which began negotiations for transfer of the land from B.C. to Environment Canada. South Moresby has initially become a national park reserve. Full control will not belong to the Canadian Parks Service until native land claims and other outstanding issues are resolved. This may take decades.

The park will ultimately include the land, the sea, and the land beneath the sea within its boundary. The perimeter runs around the southern end of Tasu Sound on Moresby Island, along the ridge of the Tangil Peninsula, and out to sea far enough that all outer islands south to Cape St. James are included. This area covers about fifteen percent of the land in the Charlotte archipelago and includes about 138 islands. These contain areas of enormous biological and cultural significance. We've chosen six spots worthy of exploration, knowing full well that you'll delight in finding additional locations of your own.

Though the park has not been officially titled, the Canadian Parks Service has initially adopted the name South Moresby/Gwaii Haanas. The latter part of the name means "place of wonder." While our information is accurate to presstime, this region of the Queen Charlotte Islands will see rapid change in the immediate future. Millions of dollars are slated to provide new visitor facilities and services. Extensive public consultation will be held before planning is completed by 1991. Presently planned are information centres in Charlotte and Sandspit, a small-boat harbour at Sandspit, and a campground with boating facilities near Moresby Camp. Smaller warden developments, imposition of park regulations, and removal of buildings will occur soon within South Moresby boundaries. Before setting out, visit the Travel Infocentre in Charlotte for current

South Moresby National Park Reserve
(showing chapter locations)

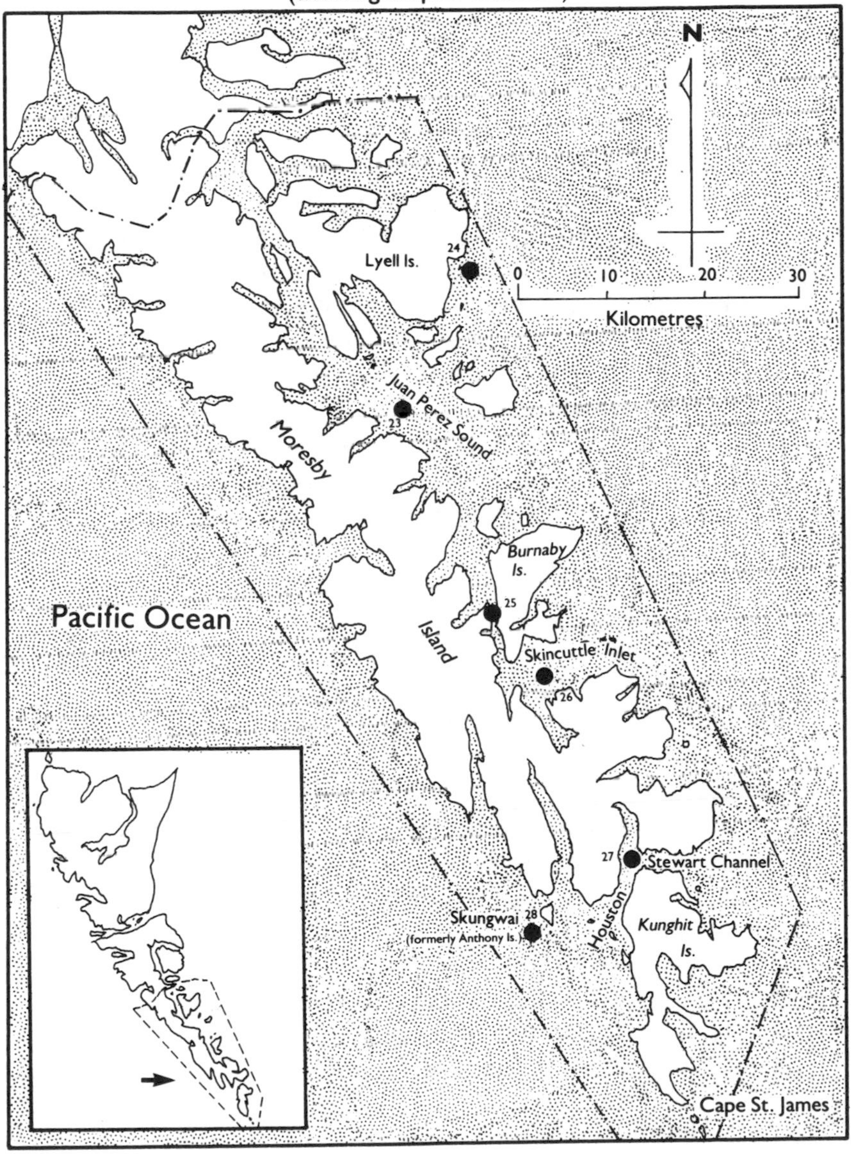

N

Lyell Is. 24

0   10   20   30
Kilometres

Juan Perez Sound
23

Moresby

Pacific Ocean

Burnaby
Is.

25

Island

Skincuttle Inlet

26

Stewart Channel
27

Skungwai 28
(formerly Anthony Is.)

Houston

Kunghit
Is.

Cape St. James

information. It's listed under **Communities** in Chapter 1.

South Moresby has no maintained roads, trails, or developments. The only access is by air or water. Anyone planning a trip here should be conscious that there are no public services south of Sandspit. People are living legally within the park proposal, so an invitation should be extended before you go ashore at their locations. In addition, Haida watchmen spend the summer at Hotspring Island, and Skedans and Ninstints Villages. In the event of an emergency, all of these people as well as park wardens have radios.

Obviously, recreationists organizing their own tour of South Moresby must be completely self-sufficient. Information useful for planning such a trip is contained in the initial portion of this book. If you are kayaking, you should allow for two weeks of daily moves to go from Moresby Camp (see **Louise Island Circumnavigation**) to Ninstints Village. That's a lot of work, and since the logged inlets of northern Moresby Island have less appeal, we recommend that you start by flying or chartering a boat to the abandoned village of Tanu or to Juan Perez Sound. By travelling southward, you'll avoid prevailing winds. By the way, it is possible to canoe here; the Haida were most successful at it. Canoeists should allow extra time for waiting out poor weather and carry a spray cover.

Motorized boats launched at Moresby Camp can go as far south as Lyell Island within a day. They still must carry enough gas to make the return trip. Inflatables have an advantage over hard hulls as they are generally more seaworthy and can be loaded into aircraft or other boats.

Kayaks can be rented on the islands, but if you're a novice with these craft, we recommend you join with experienced guides. Six paddling companies presently offer trips from June to September. There are an equal number of yachts and sailboats offering more luxurious tours on a broader season. They often have acclaimed specialists as guides. Most of these companies have their headquarters in the cities of Vancouver or Victoria, B.C. Some advertise in national outdoor magazines and a Tourism B.C. booklet, *Outdoor and Adventure Vacations*. Call 1-800-663-6000 (toll-free) for a free copy.

As a final caution, don't be disappointed if you don't find true wilderness in South Moresby. It is not a pristine environment. In our opinion it's better called a wildland because it shows many marks of contemporary development. Many islands on the east coast show

Kayak dinner on a beach. Tour leader and chef Dugald Nasmith of Pacific Rim Paddling Company rates his Teriyaki rockfish as the evening's piece de resistance.

signs of previous habitation or industry which began as early as the turn of this century. These sites don't necessarily detract from the area's attractiveness; in fact, many are of interest. You will likely also find other visitors at them. We feel very strongly that this area deserved national park status and that all Canadians should be proud that they saved it from further exploitation.

For further information:

Superintendent
South Moresby National Park Reserve
Box 37
Queen Charlotte City, B.C. V0T 1S0
Telephone: (604) 559-8818

or: Regional Director General
Canadian Parks Service, Western Region
520-220 Fourth Avenue S.E.
Calgary, Alberta T2P 3H8
Telephone: (403) 292-4401

23. Juan Perez and Darwin Sounds

Getting There

This widespread area is accessible to all aircraft and boats. Yachters can moor near Shuttle Island (one buoy only), in a tiny cove on the largest island in the Bischof group (a small log float), and at additional buoys in northern coves on Ramsay (2) and Murchison islands (3). An additional three buoys are in Section Cove on Burnaby Island.

Haida Gwaii Watchmen have a cabin on Hotspring Island, and others are open to public use. Though this island was not a traditional site for Haida, and is not an Indian reserve, they are asking visitors to show permits to land here. Camping on Hotspring is in designated areas only.

Juan Perez Sound is a wide body of water lying east of Moresby Island and south of Lyell Island. This sound and its protected passage, Darwin Sound, are probably the busiest waters in the South Moresby region. From March through to September, both commercial and recreational boats visit the area, and Hotspring Island is a 'must-do' for everyone. This region has many interesting places. The cabins and baths at Hotspring Island are a perfect base from which to explore.

The shores of the sounds are very rugged, and the mountains behind equally so. The combination of land forms and perspectives creates the most pleasing scenery we've found in the Charlottes. Even when it reverts to black and white on a rainy day, it's attractive. With the confusion of colour removed, you can better see subtle qualities of line and texture.

On one such Misty Isles day we motored into Anna Inlet on Darwin Sound. Clouds all but obscured the 1020 m (3400 ft) summits that encompassed us. One could easily imagine valkyries living among the shrouded crags above. The quiet of the inlet was calming, the surface of the water dimpled only here and there by diving birds going about their business. Ashore, the former mining community of Lockeport lay wrapped around with grassy meadows

158

Darwin Sound to Juan Perez Sound

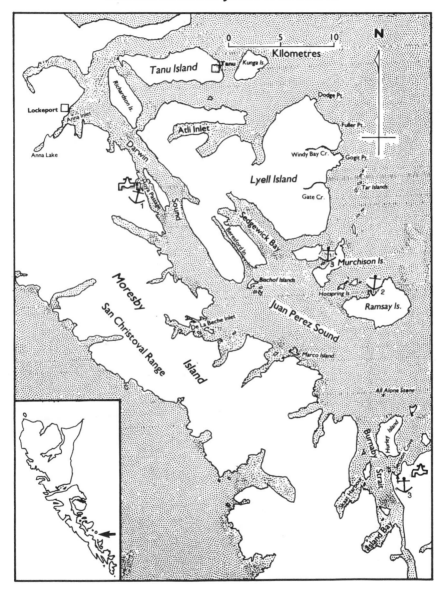

and backed by a pretty alder forest. Anna Creek tumbled down like wine spilled by the Norse gods. The crisp, cold water tasted good.

A steep trail leads up alongside the creek to Anna Lake. We needed gumboots and forty minutes to climb the 158 m (521 ft) elevation gain along a rotting boardwalk. This hazard requires nimble footwork and steady balance. Anna Lake is a tarn, it fills a glacier-carved hollow. There are, however, no glaciers left in these mountains today.

After the convenient camping at Lockeport, you'll be hard pressed to find suitable spots in Darwin Sound. Bedrock lines most of the shore, the bush has few clearings and plenty of bugs. The cove on Shuttle Island can be used as a camp in a pinch. In the opposite bay on Moresby Island, water gushes from a plastic pipe tied to a log float. Yachters should top up their water tanks here, as no better places exist further south.

The geology of this area was first surveyed by George Dawson in 1878. He was an extraordinary Canadian. His reputation is huge, and his writings are still standard references for researchers. The surnames applied to this region — Darwin, Lyell, Ramsay, Murchison, Faraday, Sedgewick, Richardson, and Bischof — were geologists or scientists whom he admired.

K.G. Bischof was a German geochemist. The tiny islands named after him are clustered in an open circle within Juan Perez Sound. Rugged and attractive, they provide temporary shelter for boats waiting to cross Juan Perez Sound. There is a spot for camping, though it's trashy and has no water. You may like to supplement your meals with the abundant abalone and bottomfish found among these islets.

Immediately north of the Bischofs is Beresford Inlet. This long narrow inlet is the result of a geological fault running along its entire length. Fresh water can be taken from creeks at its head if you happen to run out while on the Bischofs. Watch for strong tidal currents and hidden rocks in the inlet.

De La Beche was an English geologist. A rugged inlet and an island which tear into the coast of Moresby Island commemorate his name. Behind them the San Christoval Range rises 1800 m (5940 ft) to face Juan Perez Sound. These mountains are sparsely treed and their summits close to the shore. Consequently their semi-open rock slopes make for relatively quick ascents. Even though no trails lead to the peaks, this is one of the better places to get to the high country in the Charlottes.

De La Beche Inlet offers pretty boating, but is unsuited for camping as there are no beaches. Skittagetan Lagoon has dangerous rocks, as have other locations. Even in the very protected harbour of Sac Bay, the 30 m (100 ft) yacht Tom was aboard dragged anchor while everyone slept. No one awoke until the hull bumped a rock at the bay's entrance. Strong downdrafts called williwaws had blown the vessel. Fortunately no damage was done. Since these winds are so unpredictable, yachters should always set two anchors in similar situations.

For short hikes, boaters frequently visit the unnamed lakes above Sac Bay and Haswell Bay. Pull on your gumboots as no defined trails lead over the boggy ground. Enthusiasts will want to continue up the open rock slopes to the ridge of the San Christovals for a fantastic view of Juan Perez Sound.

Further south, a beach and stream hidden behind Marco Island provide good camping. Kayakers and small-boaters can wait here for better conditions before crossing to Hotspring Island. As you start out, watch for seals hauled out on rocks at the east end of Marco Island.

Hotspring is an island of 8 ha (20 a) with a group of warm springs which have fortuitously come to the surface here rather than on the seabed. They seep from bedrock at four locations. Their temperature varies, even day to day. Pool temperatures range between 52° C and 76° C (125-168° F). The strongly mineralized water is of no benefit to drink. However, Francis Poole's book tells that Haida Chief Klue believed the hot pools were a cure for all diseases. One of Poole's own men returned from "Volcanic Island" having remedied his rheumatic fever. These claims of the restorative powers of hotsprings are identical to those of spas the world over.

Most of Hotspring's devotees simply want a bath. But what a difficult choice! This seaside spa offers pools ranging from a tiny shrub-enclosed *sitzbath* to an exposed iron bathtub. Soap or shampoo should be used only in the covered tubs since they otherwise accumulate in the natural pools. Three outdoor basins look onto the superb Juan Perez vista. Passing squalls, wave patterns, boats, and birds constantly redesign this scene. A field companion likened it to living within a Toni Onley painting. Watching this while up to your neck in hot water, as the sun slides over the San Christovals, has to be the *piece de resistance* experience of the southern Charlottes.

Hotspring Island offers other comforts atypical of a wildland.

161

A solitary soak in the natural spa of Hotspring Island is rare due to its summer popularity. A gregarious bather might rub elbows with Haida, fishermen, New York financiers or internationally-known conservationists.

Three simple cabins have been constructed. The public may use two, although one is for preferential use by Haida tours. Such facilities tend to attract parties, so those wanting to avoid the crowd will have to camp on the beachfront or at either end of the island where pit toilets have been constructed. Trails connect these campsites to the springs. Another trail leads to an enclosed seep which produces the only drinking water on this island. You will find this shallow well near the east end.

The pools of Hotspring are enjoyed most when few people are about (particularly for skinny-dipping). But constant boat and aircraft traffic can be detracting. Campers will find quieter sites on House Island (connected to Hotspring at low tide) and nearby Ramsay Island. Still, we've always managed to find special moments between the comings and goings. Once we bathed late, placing candles in a poolside grotto. They cast a flickering glow over the faces of our friends, and silhouetted the fringing shrubbery against the stars. A breeze wafted the mist in tapers off the water, momentarily obscuring our companions. Small bats flitted boldly between us, picking insects from the surface. The talk was small, but the feelings of connectedness strong. It was one of those mellowing times when one is at peace with the world. The hotsprings may not cure physical ailments, but they sure restored our psyche.

24.   East Coast of Lyell Island

Getting There

Windy Bay Creek, on the east coast of Lyell Island, remains unmarked on topographic maps or marine charts. Located between Gogit Point and Fuller Point, it is accessible to helicopters and boats. You may stay in the Blinking Eye House unless Haida tours are present. Undeveloped campsites also exist near the house.

Many people consider Lyell Island the centrepiece of the South Moresby region. It was here that Haida and environmental activists concentrated their field protests during the controversy to save the region from logging. Pictures of Lyell Island clear-cuts first brought the attention of most Canadians to the issues involved in the national park proposal. National media covered the Haida being arrested in 1985 for blocking access to the loggers. Although northern and eastern portions of the island were extensively clear-cut before the success of the protest groups, the Windy Bay watershed and Dodge Point were saved from the saw. Lyell Island and smaller satellite islands to the east are worthy of a day's exploration.

Windy Bay is identified by its position between Gogit and Fuller Points. It's an exposed location, and passage along the outside of Lyell Island should not be attempted in poor or threatening weather. Strong tides run past both points.

If you are storm-bound here, there is good camping with fresh water available from the creek. If you choose roofed shelter, Blinking Eye House is of modified traditional design built by the Haida, with wooden sleeping platforms and a gravel floor. It was officially opened in 1987. Windy Bay is also the site of an ancient village, and remnants of former houses can be found. These natives had access to the stands of magnificent trees immediately behind. It was this rainforest which inspired the fight to save South Moresby. Its beauty was recognized early.

In 1900 biologist William Osgood spent five weeks studying the flora and fauna of these islands. Writing about the rainforest, he said, ". . . the spruces stand in magnificent groves, the grandeur of

163

A tall Sitka spruce (*Picea sitchensis*) in Windy Bay watershed. These valuable trees now compose only two percent of British Columbia's old-growth forests. The Haida wove spruce roots into waterproof hats.

which is appreciated only when one gets above the tangle of underbrush and obtains an unobstructed view of the tall, straight, reddish barked trunks, column after column extending far back into the forest, until the dim light is finally obscured and individual trees can no longer be distinguished.''

It sounds rather like the Parthenon, and Windy Bay is certainly a temple of nature. Here no undergrowth obstructs movement; a deep carpet of moss invites your tread across the forest floor. To step off the trail for a moment alone is humbling, yet inspiring. The trees are so big one feels insignificant creeping over their spreading roots. The cedars in this valley rise to 70 m (230 ft). Nearing 1000 years of age, some are among the oldest organisms living in this country.

Little direct sunlight penetrates below the forest canopy. Sounds are muffled. Occasionally the song of some small bird faintly reaches your ear. You might recognize the call of Townsend's Warbler, Golden-crowned Kinglet, or Chestnut-backed Chickadee. Other bird calls carry surprisingly well. The double bell tone of a Common Raven resonates through the trunks 'dong-dong'. From the sky above a Bald Eagle cries its creaky stutter. It's easy to hear why the Haida attributed supernatural qualities to the latter two birds.

The natives came into these woods to cut the western redcedar. The trees grow to great sizes in these moist woods, and many show the scars of native use. Such trees may have some of their bark stripped off or have been 'holed' in a test for internal rot. There is no way to locate specific specimens, so you'll have to make your own wandering discoveries. A trail does wind parallel to the creek, but if

Examining an old Haida test hole in a wester redcedar (*Thuja plicata*) trunk in Windy Bay watershed. Trees of this size became canoes or house timbers. Evidently this specimen was found unsuitable.

you deviate from it have a good sense of direction or carry a compass. It is very easy to become disoriented in these woods.

Among the buttressed bases you will find cedars with scars where bark has been removed. Haida women collected the bark by making horizontal cuts, then pulling out, ripping strips up the trunk. They separated the fibres and wove them into clothing and various coverings. The soft bark was also made into rope, fishnets, baskets, and numerous items of a twined or woven nature.

Cedars at Windy Bay were also cut down for construction material. It was the men who sought large straight trees for house timbers, canoes, and totem poles. A tree was not cut until it had been tested for core rot. Once selected, trees were taken down by chipping and/or burning. We discovered one horizontal log which had been partially cut into boards.

There is so much evidence of primitive logging in this watershed that is has been called a "living museum." Cedar was a multiple-purpose material for the Haida, and virtually their exclusive choice of wood. It is soft, light, straight-grained, easy to split, and holds paint well. It also contains a fragrant natural oil which makes it resistant to decay, even in the sodden Northwest Coast climate.

Cedar was the wood of life for the Haida just as surely as salmon was the food of life. Windy Bay Creek is the largest and most productive spawning stream in South Moresby. When fall rains raise water levels, pink and coho salmon return to lay eggs in the gravel which birthed them. Pinks are the most abundant. In late September their numbers are estimated at over 55,000. Coho complete their life cycle from late October through November.

Five kilometres (3 mi) to the north on Dodge Point is another annual breeding concentration. Here is South Moresby's largest known breeding colony of Ancient Murrelets. Initially estimated at 60,000 pairs, their numbers are expanding, due in part to the ideal habitat of Lyell Island's rainforest. Murrelets need the spaced trees and open floors of old-growth forests as they become grounded if obstructed by low-level vegetation. They need lots of open space to manoeuvre around tree trunks. Among the roots of a mature spruce and cedar, these birds nest in underground burrows.

In late March adults return to the colony and select burrows within sight of the sea. After hatching, young birds are better able to orient themselves when emerging from the underground chamber. The lack of vegetation helps these flightless fluffballs make their way to the waters edge. Once on the water the chicks head out to sea under the cover of darkness. Congregations of thousands raft together 2 - 6 km (1 - 4 mi) offshore. Look for them near Tuft Islets at the end of May or early in June.

All the islands off the east coast of Lyell are good places to see varied marine fauna. The Tar Islands are used frequently by seals for haul-outs. Killer whales know this and often cruise this coast for prey. We encountered one transient group of five orca while on Agglomerate Island, and were privileged witnesses to a very special display.

While we stood transfixed on the edge of a cliff that rose only a few feet above the water, the whales engaged in seemingly spontaneous playful behaviour literally beneath our feet. For a full thirty minutes these magnificent marine mammals interacted with one another, and with us. They swam in gentle contorted patterns around one another, rubbed against kelp stalks, and spyhopped (raised their heads straight out of the water) to check our activity on shore, all of this within 6 m (20 ft) of where we stood. Finally, after their engaging performance, it seemed our turn, and the whales lay on the surface of the water to listen while we tried to entertain them with song.

When at last they departed, it seemed only because we had exhausted our meagre repertoire of antics. We were frustrated by our inability to communicate with these intelligent mammals. Yet there was no doubt but that they had chosen to spend time in our presence. We felt oddly special, and grateful. That day on the eastern coast of Lyell Island will always be a highlight of our Charlotte experiences.

25. Burnaby Narrows

Getting There

This strait is accessible to helicopters and boats. Motorboats will have difficult passing through the channel at low tide, but markers aid navigation at high water. Large craft can anchor north or south of the narrows or in nearby bays. Yachters will find a slow-flowing fresh water pipe and three mooring buoys in Section Cove on northern Burnaby Island.

Burnaby Strait connects the waters of Juan Perez Sound and Skincuttle Inlet. The strait tapers to a 50 m (165 ft) width that charts and maps label as Dolomite Narrows, but the local name of Burnaby Narrows is so widely used that we have used it instead. This spot is excellent for seeing intertidal life as well as for use as a base camp to explore the inlets on either end of Burnaby Strait.

At the narrows are the remains of several shacks dating from the 'hippie' era of the late 60's and early 70's. Only one of them provides reasonable shelter, but it is infested with mice. Pretty shoreline meadows surrounding these old abodes make better campsites. In early June Pacific crab apple trees will be blossoming beside your tent. Firewood can be found in the forest and fresh water flows in several adjacent creeks. If they're dry, a large stream in nearby Island Bay has clear water.

If you plan to stay here, check a tide table. During our last trip, low tide occurred at 6:00 a.m. Determined to make the most of our time, we awakened at first light. We pulled on gumboots and carried cameras and field guides along to the shallows. Scrambling down the pebble beach we encountered raccoons, eagles, and ravens foraging breakfast.

You'll find it almost impossible to walk here without stepping on something alive. The abundance is due to the strong tidal action through the narrows which brings a constant supply of nutrients to these creatures. Most are filter-feeders including clams, barnacles, and mussels. They strain the water with special brushes called cirri, which trap minute free-floating organisms. Equally conspicuous sea

Bat stars (*Patiria miniata*) and butter clams (*Saxidomus giganteus*) in Burnaby
Narrows. The concentration of marine life here is supported by high nutrient
turnover in the strong tidal fluctuations.

stars blanket the bottom like a tapestry resembling the heavens.
Each has a different colour, and when surrounded by textured
algae, provide terrific photographic compositions.

After further looking you may notice curious mounds in the mud,
or a sandy-coloured ring resembling a rubber toilet plunger. Both
are created by the large, spherical moon snail. This carnivorous
shellfish ploughs beneath the surface in search of clams, which it
envelopes with its fleshy foot. Once trapped, a small hole is rasped
through the clamshell allowing access to its innards. The purpose of
the rubbery rings still puzzles many people. They are used for
reproduction. As the snails extrude their eggs in a gelatinous sheet,
sand binds to the sticky mass. A thin collar forms around the shape
of the shell, hardens, then splits. The grey ring remains on top of the
muddy bottom. About mid-summer this egg case breaks down
releasing thousands of free-swimming moon snail larvae.

Red rock crabs also live here. These crustaceans are smaller and
have less meat than the commercially-favoured Dungeness crab.
Their black-tipped pincers have considerable strength, adding new
meaning to the term "armed and dangerous." Tom discovered this
when demonstrating the method of capturing crabs by hand. Using
approved technique, he grasped the shell from the rear. His

168

The meadow on Burnaby Island at the narrows has ideal camping with fresh
water, firewood and a rudimentary shelter. The opportunity for easy food may
attract bears, so the usual overnight precautions must be taken.

specimen was unusually agile, and deftly pinched his index finger
with the strength of a vice. Blood, pincer, and crab flew in different
directions as he recoiled in pain. Clenched teeth later gave way to a
smug smile as he cracked open the dismembered limbs and savoured
the tasty meat of the culprit.

Only the tide will limit your time in this exciting area. After water
floods the shallows, set out to explore nearby bays and coves. To the
immediate south, Bag Harbour is the site of a former Haida village.
The remnants of several salmon weirs can be seen in the bed of the
stream which enters here. A clam cannery operated between 1908
and 1910. A rusted boiler and a heap of shells remain along the
shore. Although one of the richest shellfish beds on our Pacific
coast, these clams can no longer be eaten. Burnaby Narrows has, for
unknown reasons, unusually high levels of toxins which cause
paralytic shellfish poisoning, or red tide. For this reason, the
harvesting of shellfish (except razor clams) is permanently
prohibited here and throughout the Charlottes.

North of the narrows is a large opening into Island Bay. Enter
with your motor at dead slow and chart in hand, for the bay is
guarded by seventeen islands and at least as many rocks. All of these
provide a picturesque foreground to Yatza Mountain, part of the

San Christoval Range. On clear days its summit provides fine views, though no defined trails lead to the top. A cascade at the far end of Island Bay offers a refreshing drink and a place to fill water containers. In 1961 the carcass of a great white shark discovered here was the first recorded in B.C. Over a dozen other great whites have been found washed ashore on the Charlottes since.

Further north, Burnaby Strait gradually widens. On the northwest corner of Burnaby Island, Section Cove has reasonable camping, fresh water, and a sandy beach. Here you will find logs chained together to form floating pens anchored near shore. These booms form part of a traditional native fishery for Pacific herring spawn. In spring large blades of the kelp *Macrocystis* hang from the logs. As herring gather in huge schools, the raft and suspended kelp are pushed into concentrations of the spawning fish. The herring lay small white eggs directly on the kelp, sometimes several layers deep. The resulting algal caviar, known as gow, is a delicacy for native people and the Japanese. Gow may be eaten raw, quick fried, or dried. In 1987 the industry throughout B.C. generated over ten million dollars in overseas sales.

Every trip into South Moresby should include at least a full day in Burnaby Narrows. It will be a memorable time, particularly if you can coincide your visit during the zero or minus tides of the summer months.

26. Skincuttle Inlet

Getting There

This large inlet is accessible to all aircraft and boats. Yachters will find mooring buoys in Jedway Bay and can anchor in many other places, but Harriet Harbour is not recommended for overnight. Avoid landing on East Copper and Jeffrey islands which form an ecological reserve for seabirds.

Skincuttle Inlet is a 6 km (3.7 mi) wide opening onto Hecate Strait between Burnaby and Moresby islands. Within the inlet are five scattered groups of smaller islands. Many inlets, bays, and a strait convolute the shoreline into attractive anchorages. Surrounding hills rise to 350 m (1155 ft) and form a solid wooded aspect. Low tides expose interesting rocks along the shoreline, on the smallest islands, and above Harriet Harbour.

Anyone interested in minerals or geology will enjoy several days of exploration in Skincuttle Inlet. Mining here dates back to 1862. You'll find huge open pits, the remains of three mining communities, and several underground tunnels. There is an interesting landform, and remains of a former cannery and nearby commune.

Jedway was first established in the early 1900s when prospectors were attracted by copper deposits. Although the miners searched throughout the inlet, their home base was along the west side of Harriet Harbour. This townsite included two wharfs, a sawmill, and numerous cabins. After eight decades little remains as the site is completely overgrown. Even here antique bottle diggers have scavenged the dump.

Above Harriet Harbour waste rock forms a loose slope below an open pit. Pieces of heavy magnetite, a rich ore of iron, still litter the ground. This rock will attract a magnet. Jedway was one of two iron ore mines in the Charlottes which formerly shipped concentrate to Japanese steel mills (the other was at Tasu on the west coast of Moresby Island). Jedway operated between 1961 and 1968, employing 130 full-time staff.

The Haida name for this pretty bay was "gigawai," meaning

Skincuttle Inlet to Houston Stewart Channel

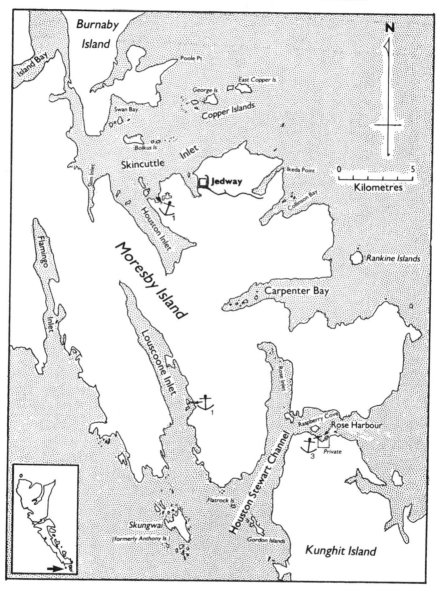

trap. Modern mariners still need to beware its hazards. The magnetite will deflect navigational compasses, so use caution if moving under limited visibility. Industrial sites such as this commonly dumped scrap metal in the sea. Your anchor could snag bottom debris. Also this seemingly-protected bay is prone to strong southerly downdrafts. A small island opposite a large dock provides some protection for boats while you go ashore. The townsite of Jedway has been well cleaned away, but the roads leading to the mines are still open for walking. The least obstructed route parallels the harbour before leading uphill. It will take slow walkers two hours to reach the ridge between Jedway and Ikeda Cove. This vantage offers fine sunset views of Skincuttle Inlet.

From the ridge the road descends toward Ikeda Cove but doesn't reach the water. It goes to additional workings on the south slope. During construction of this road the workings of an earlier copper mine were partially obliterated. Watch along the upper side for a mine portal and dump piles of this 1906-1920 operation managed by Arichika Ikeda, a successful Japanese businessman.

Ore from his mines was shipped to a smelter on Vancouver Island. In the piles left at the ore bunkers you can find chalcopyrite. This brassy mineral is sometimes called copper pyrite. After hand sorting, ore was carted to the loading wharf on a one-metre gauge tramway. From the road's lowest point, you can follow the rails to the old camp at the water's edge.

Water from any of these mines is safe to drink, but avoid the settling pond at Jedway. It may still contain harmful chemicals. Fresh water can also be obtained from streams which run into Harriet Harbour or nearby at Jedway Bay. Boaters can fill their tanks at the end of that bay where fresh water flows slowly from a plastic pipe.

Also at Jedway Bay are remains of a Japanese abalone cannery. In the woods behind the rotting buildings is a touching inscription on a wooden grave marker. The grave of Mrs. Taniyo Isozaki dates from the dark decades when Japanese were ostracized by the 'white' community. Sadly, we know nothing of her or the cannery operations.

By contrast, we know much about the first European resident in Skincuttle Inlet, Francis Poole. This English engineer was prospecting for copper here in 1862-63. He later published his explorations in *Queen Charlotte Islands: A Narrative of Discovery and Adventure in the North Pacific*. Poole's venture failed, his

The flooding horseshoe cavern at Poole Point. One end opens on the sea, the other on land. It has been eroded into granite-like rocks by waves. Landings are possible only during a calm sea.

miners mutinied, and his life was threatened several times. But he still wrote appreciatively of the Charlottes: "I stood by the beach for fully half an hour, thinking how difficult it would be to find a sweeter spot in all the world, and how at no distant date that very beach would assuredly give way to the wharves and landing-places of a flourishing commercial town. Harriet Harbour has only to be known in order to be seized upon in the interests of trade and colonization."

But Poole never followed this vision. His mines were located in the limestone on Copper Islands and at Pelican Cove on Burnaby Island. Despite his quest for copper, he was never successful. Old shafts and camp remains are still visible at the sites where he laboured.

Poole Point on Burnaby Island is named after him, but the holes here are from erosion, not mining. This point is subject to strong winds and landing is difficult on the stony beaches. Those who do get ashore will be fascinated by the cave. Heavy seas have carved the granitic rocks into a horseshoe cavern with two openings onto the same shore. The major opening gapes ten metres by six (33 x 20 ft). The adjacent hole has a partially-collapsed ceiling, creating a separated arch. At low tide you can kayak into the flooded passage, though ocean surges can make it dangerous. Around the arch's base, the sea swirls stones which grind circular holes in the bedrock. Such grinders are called millstones, and the depressions, pot-holes.

Also on Burnaby Island, five shacks at Swan Bay are of minor interest. This idyllic setting was the homesite of people seeking an alternate lifestyle. They struggled for six or seven years before deciding that the financial cost and their children's education made civilization more attractive. Many such groups and individuals tried to survive in the South Moresby region, but few had long-term success. Despite the ideals of the back-to-the-land movement, in the final analysis they were poorer caretakers than their industrial neighbours across the inlet, who at least cleaned camp before departing.

Today we can all contribute positively to a wiser and more responsible vision of the future by supporting the creation of park lands such as South Moresby. We hope that its preservation will inspire visitors to return home with the desire for better conservation of their local environments.

27. Houston Stewart Channel

Getting There

Houston Stewart Channel separates Moresby Island from smaller Kunghit Island to the south. The channel is accessible to aircraft and boats, and three mooring buoys are provided in Rose Harbour. There is another on the east side of nearby Louscoone Inlet. Charter flights originating from Sandspit often land in Louscoone Inlet as it's a shorter distance and cheaper than flying into Houston Stewart Channel.

Tidal currents of seven knots push through the channel between the Pacific Ocean and Hecate Strait. Beware of standing waves caused by such strong tides at Point Langford at the eastern end of Houston Stewart Channel. Private property at Rose Harbour is open for bed and breakfast. See map, page 172.

Many people begin or complete their South Moresby explorations in Houston Stewart Channel since the area is as far south as most groups go. The channel has suitable pick-up and drop-off places, offers refuge from poor weather, and is close to a major place of interest — Ninstints Village, a UNESCO World Heritage Site.

Early sailing ships used Houston Stewart Channel for similar reasons, anchoring here on trading visits. At first they conducted commerce with the natives without problems, but eventually hostilities broke out. At least four ships were attacked, and two were burned. There was considerable loss of life to both Haida and traders. These tragic events are retold from a native perspective in Christie Harris' novel *Raven's Cry*.

In 1853 sailors aboard the *Virago* mentioned finding fresh stream water on the north side of the channel. They also found lush red salmonberries which they called raspberries. Now known as Raspberry Cove, this location is a good campsite. Unfortunately, minute biting flies called no-see-ums have discovered the area as well.

Directly across from the campsite is Rose Harbour. This former whaling station operated between 1910 and 1942, employing up to a hundred men seasonally. Management even brought in their

Photo courtesy Raine family collection.

A 24 m (81 ft) blue whale (*Balaenoptera musculus*) on the flensing deck at Rose Harbour in September 1918. The blue whale is the largest animal ever to live on earth. This specimen produced over 370 drums of oil.

families for the summer. Records indicate that over 2000 whales were processed and shipped out as barrels of oil, mink food, and fertilizer. The foul smell generated a lot of wisecracks about the facility's floral name. In fact, it was called after the same George Rose whose name is applied to Nai-Kun (Rose Spit).

The whaling company eventually went bankrupt and most of its machinery was dismantled. An anecdotal history of whaling here and on Graham Island has been written by W.A. Hagelund in *Whalers No More*. On the beach at Rose Harbour rust two digesters which rendered whale blubber and bones. A plain monument nearby is dedicated to Oriental workers who died while employed here. Boilers which provided steam remain hidden behind the trees and modern buildings. Several homes are now built on the site. Families have resided here since 1978, living off the land and sea. They've come a long way to find privacy.

A pleasant trip ashore can be made nearby in five kilometre-long (3 mi) Rose Inlet. Inflatables and kayaks require careful navigation through rocks and kelp to reach the broad salt marsh at the inlet's terminus. Such a large foraging area is rare in South Moresby, making this important habitat. Deer and bear graze in the meadow, and it's also popular with migrating waterfowl.

Beyond the western end of Rose Inlet all that exists between you and the Pacific horizon are small island clusters. Despite its name this ocean is rarely pacific, and boaters should be properly equipped and cognizant of its dangers before travelling out here. For this reason the western side of Kunghit Island is infrequently visited.

At the very mouth of the channel is Flatrock Island, a mesa-topped monolith which supports Glaucous-winged Gull and Pelagic Cormorant nesting colonies. Rocky ramparts make landings difficult. Nearby Gordon Islands have some pretty nooks which only kayakers can easily navigate. Such a remote coastal location offers the possibility of finding Japanese glass balls. The best-known island cluster contains Skungwai (formerly Anthony Island), location of Ninstints, described in the next chapter.

Around Skungwai, smaller islets are excellent for locating birds. Nine of the thirteen species of seabirds which breed in B.C. nest in this one group — an estimated 35,000 pairs. They utilize every type of available habitat — burrows, rock crevices, and on open rock or thin vegetation. British Columbia's first nesting record of a Horned Puffin was made here. Our favourite is the Tufted Puffin. Their colourful faces, fat bodies, and wings which seem to revolve around their mid-section give them the resemblance of stunt planes at an air show. Islets all around Skungwai are an ecological reserve to protect these birds, so remain in your boat while exploring and birdwatching.

This is a great area to see mammals as well. Steller sea lions rest on the outermost rocks exposed to surf and spray. Watch for harbour seals among the islets and river otters within Houston Stewart Channel. There is an exceptional diversity of submarine organisms as well.

If you're going to see whales on your trip, either end of Houston Stewart Channel is a likely locale. Watch for spouting gray and minke whales near shore, or a humpback breaching further out. Killer whales sometimes cruise right through the channel.

Houston Stewart Channel is typical of the Queen Charlottes. The whaling station, like many island enterprises, lies in rust. The wildlife is representative of the entire archipelago. Though many people see this area simply as a passage to more interesting locations, the concentration of wildlife here may not be found elsewhere. This could be your first or last opportunity to tick a species off your checklist before leaving the Charlottes.

28. Ninstints Village

Getting There

Skungwai (formerly Anthony Island) is the location of this famous abandoned Haida village. The island sits 3 km (2 mi) off the western end of Houston Stewart Channel, on the edge of the Pacific. Floatplanes will rarely land here, favouring Louscoone Inlet to the north or Houston Stewart Channel. Helicopters unfortunately land regularly on the beach directly in front of the village. Small boats may beach in front of the village or on the sheltered northeastern end of the island, from where a trail leads to the village. Permits may be purchased in Skidegate before arriving. Good campsites exist at nearby Louscoone Point and within Louscoone Inlet.

This tiny island seems an unlikely place to find the masterpieces of a culture's creative genius. Yet Anthony Island has international significance for its artistic heritage. Here stand the world's greatest totem poles still on their original ground.

The island is most appropriately referred to by the Haida name of Skungwai — Red Cod Island. Here decays Ninstints, abandoned home of 400 Haida, and formerly one of the largest villages in the South Moresby region. Archeologists have compared it favourably with the lost jungle cities of Mexico and Cambodia. It's legacy in wood was recognized in 1981 by the United Nations as a World Heritage Site. Thus it ranks with places such as Egypt's pyramids and the palace at Versailles, France. Ninstints presents an exceptional testimony to a civilization which very nearly disappeared.

This was the territory of the Kunghit, a subdivision of the Haida nation, whose territory was the South Moresby region. They occupied this site for at least 1500 years, using it as a year-round residence. During the summer people scattered throughout their territory to hunt, fish, and gather plant foods. They occupied their time in winter with carving, construction, and social ceremony, often in conjunction with other villages.

Ninstints was a difficult place for guests or enemies to approach. The winds of winter, and sometimes of summer, are among the

179

Their genius has produced monumental works of art on a par with the most original the world has ever known. They belong one and all to our continent and our time, and have shown how creative power may thrive in remote places.

Dr. Marius Barbeau, 1954
distinguished Canadian ethnologist

strongest in Canada. Yet the village itself is well-sheltered on the lee side of the island. A smaller island lies in front, restricting passage to a concealed cove behind. Here canoes once beached before numerous houses. When low tide dries the bay, you can still see canoe runs cleared through the beach cobbles. This is still the main point of access, although there is a small beach on the south side of an adjacent peninsula.

People don't say much when they arrive here. A straggling row of bestial eyes silences them. Decaying wooden faces on the totems stare out to sea as if to ignore the intrusion. You feel like asking permission of the spirits to tread among them. But the presence of the dead is strong. Perhaps it's fitting that the majority of the poles standing are mortuaries honouring the men who led this village to greatness. The bodies of dead chiefs were entombed in enclosures at the top of the poles. Other poles include tall memorials commemorating an ancestor and house poles which marked a house entrance.

Totems do not depict pagans or demons, nor were they worshipped as was often supposed. The animal and human figures on them represent family crests and mythology and are similar to European coats-of-arms or Scottish tartans. The totemic symbols make a statement about genealogy, and possibly the individual commemorated. Tragically, most of these meanings have been forgotten or lost. We are only able to identify the stylized beings.

Oddly, many of the animals symbolized on the poles weren't found on the Charlottes in those days. These include the beaver

180

(with cross-hatched tail), frog, (with toothless grin) and grizzly bear (with protruding tongue). These animals may indicate Haida familiarity with mainland hunting. Other figures are recognizable as eagles and killer whales. Some poles are virtually unrecognizable, having been damaged by a grass fire in 1892.

Of the twenty-six poles remaining at Ninstints (many have been removed to museums), five have toppled. Their decay is a natural progression. The Haida never attempted to keep them indefinitely. They might have placed a prop beneath a leaner to keep it from falling on a house or path. Once down, a pole was simply pushed aside and allowed to rot.

Decay has affected the houses more seriously. Collapsed beams and posts lie behind the poles, once forming the framework of seventeen houses. The largest of these was 14.3 m by 14.9 m (47 ft x 49 ft) and had an excavated floor. It is one of two houses here which have terraced interiors. George MacDonald's booklet *Ninstints: Haida World Heritage Site* provides excellent drawings of their design. Artist Gordon Miller has also rendered the village in exquisite detail as it appeared during its peak. Their book is a helpful on-site guide to identifying the houses and totems.

The Kunghit people suffered the most of any Haida in their early contacts with Europeans and Americans. Led by a prideful and embittered chief, they attacked four trading vessels in as many years, twice destroying entire ships and crews. During the last attempt in 1795, the chief Koyah and fifty warriors were killed with no loss to the traders. Although these incidents have long been attributed to Ninstints, the 1987 discovery of an even larger village on Kunghit Island has confirmed it as the home of the fearless chief. Following Koyah's death the Kunghit kept much to themselves for many decades.

Their isolation, however, was no protection from the new diseases whitemen brought. Smallpox first struck late in the eighteenth century, probably transmitted by Russian fur traders. A subsequent epidemic was deliberately introduced in 1862. The Haida social fabric was torn further apart when they obtained liquor, and when many of the young people moved to a decadent camp on the outskirts of Victoria on Vancouver Island. By 1884 only thirty people remained at Ninstints. Unable to support themselves, they eventually moved to Skidegate. Today there are no traceable descendents of the once-great Kunghit tribe.

The rainforest soon took over. For many years the site was entirely abandonned, forgotten. Finally, in 1978 a program of

This Haida skeleton was revealed among the roots of a windthrown spruce. The body had been left on the surface of a midden (refuse heap) hundreds of years before. Never disturb any relic and report such finds to authorities.

preventative conservation began. The plan now is to keep these poles in place and to slow their deterioration as much as possible. A native warden comes each summer to monitor visitors. There are now hundreds of visiting parties recorded each year.

This is both a blessing and a curse. While no one will argue the necessity of visitors in terms of justifying the preservation of such a site, large numbers of visitors could eventually cause detrimental impacts. For this reason, camping on the island is not permitted. Access may be denied to anyone without a permit from the Skidegate Band Council. Visitors should be very conscious about walking only on established paths. This legacy deserves your respect. Wilson Duff and Michael Kew summarized this in their 1957 *Report of the Provincial Museum*:

"A few fragments of memory, a few bright glimpses in the writings of the past, some old and weathered totem-poles in a storage shed and the moldering remnants of once-magnificent carved post and houses on the site of the old village — these are all that survive of the tribe and village chiefs Koyah and Ninstints. What was destroyed here was not just a few hundred individual human lives. Human beings must die anyway. It was something even more complex and even more human — a vigorous and functioning society, the product of just as long an evolution as our own, well suited to its environment and vital enough to participate in human cultural achievements not duplicated anywhere else. What was destroyed was one more bright tile in the complicated and wonderful mosaic of man's achievement on earth. Mankind is the loser. We are the losers."

Further Reading

Bigg, Michael, et al. *Killer Whales*. Nanaimo: Phantom Press & Publishers Inc., 1987.

Brown, A. Sutherland. *Geology of the Queen Charlotte Islands, B.C.* Victoria: Department of Mines and Petroleum Resources, bulletin 54, 1968.

Campbell, R. Wayne, et al. *Volume 1: The Birds of British Columbia — Loons through Woodpeckers*. Victoria: Royal B.C. Museum, 1989.

Carr, Emily. *Klee Wyck*. Toronto: Clarke, Irwin & Co., 1971 [c. 1941].

Carter, Jimmy. *An Outdoor Journal*. Toronto: Bantam Books, 1988.

Collison, William H. *In the Wake of the War Canoe*. Victoria: Sono Nis Press, reprint, 1981.

Dalzell, Kathleen E. *The Queen Charlotte Islands , 2 vol.* Queen Charlotte City: 1968 (*1774 -1966*); 1973 (*Book 2: Of Places and Names*).

Dawson, George M. *Report on the Queen Charlotte Islands*, including *Appendix A: On the Haida Indians* Montreal: Geological Survey of Canada, 1880.

Duff, Wilson and Michael Kew. "Anthony Island, A Home of the Haidas", *Report of the Provincial Museum. Victoria: Provincial Museum*, 1957.

Green, David and Wayne Campbell. *The Amphibians of B.C.* Victoria: B.C. Provincial Museum Handbook 45, 1984.

Gregory, Patrick and Wayne Campbell, *The Reptiles of B.C.* Victoria: B.C. Provincial Museum Handbook 44, 1984.

Hagelund, William A. *Whalers No More*. Madeira Park: Harbour Publishing, 1987.

Haley, Delphine (ed.). *Marine Mammals*. Seattle: Pacific Search Press, 1986.

Harris, Christie. *Raven's Cry*. Toronto: McClelland and Stewart, 1966.

Islands Protection Society. *Islands at the Edge: Preserving the Queen Charlotte Islands Wilderness*. Vancouver: Douglas and McIntyre, 1984.

Long, Bob. *Fishing the Queen Charlotte Islands*. Sandspit: Rasen Enterprises Ltd., 1988.

MacDonald, George F. *Ninstints: Haida World Heritage Site*. Vancouver: University of British Columbia Press, 1983.

Osgood, Wilfred H. *Natural History of the Queen Charlotte Islands, B.C.* Washington: Government Printing Office, 1901.

Poole, Francis. *Queen Charlotte Islands: A Narrative of Discovery and Adventure in the North Pacific*. London: Hurst and Blackett, 1872; reprinted Vancouver: J.J. Douglas, 1972.

Sheldon, Charles. *The Wilderness of the North Pacific Coast Islands*. New York: Charles Scribner's Sons, 1912.

Smyly, John and Smyly, Carolyn. *Those Born at Koona*. Vancouver: Hancock House, 1973.

South Moresby Resource Planning Team. *South Moresby Land Use Alternatives*. Victoria: Queen's Printer, 1983.

Stewart, Hilary. *Cedar*. Vancouver: Douglas and McIntyre, 1984.

BIRDS OF THE QUEEN CHARLOTTE ISLANDS

Br — Breeding Sp — Spring Su — Summer Fa — Fall Wi — Winter
• — denotes breeding or occurrence in season

	Br	Sp	Su	Fa	Wi	
Red-throated Loon	•	•	•	•	•	
Pacific Loon		•	•	•	•	
Common Loon	•	•	•	•	•	
Yellow-billed Loon		•	•	•	•	
Pied-billed Grebe		•			•	
Horned Grebe		•	•	•	•	
Red-necked Grebe		•	•	•	•	
Eared Grebe		•	•	•	•	
Western Grebe		•	•	•	•	
Black-footed Albatross		•	•	•		
Laysan Albatross		•	•	•		
Northern Fulmar		•	•		•	
Pink-footed Shearwater		•	•	•	•	
Flesh-footed Shearwater		•				
Buller's Shearwater			•	•		
Sooty Shearwater		•	•	•		
Short-tailed Shearwater		•	•	•	•	
Fork-tailed Storm-Petrel	•	•	•	•	•	
Leach's Storm-Petrel	•	•	•	•	•	
Double-crested Cormorant		•	•	•	•	
Brandt's Cormorant		•	•	•	•	
Pelagic Cormorant	•	•	•	•	•	
Red-faced Cormorant			•			
Magnificent Frigatebird			•			
American Bittern		•			•	
Great Blue Heron	•	•	•	•	•	
Great Egret				•		
Cattle Egret		•		•	•	
Tundra Swan		•	•	•	•	
Trumpeter Swan		•	•	•	•	
Greater-White-fronted Goose		•	•	•	•	
Snow Goose		•	•	•	•	

	Br	Sp	Su	Fa	Wi	
Emperor Goose		•		•	•	
Brant		•	•	•	•	
Canada Goose	•	•	•	•	•	
Wood Duck		•		•	•	
Green-winged Teal	•	•	•	•	•	
Mallard	•	•	•	•	•	
Northern Pintail	•	•	•	•	•	
Blue-winged Teal	•	•	•	•	•	
Cinnamon Teal		•	•		•	
Northern Shoveler		•	•	•	•	
Gadwall		•	•	•	•	
Eurasian Wigeon		•		•	•	
American Wigeon		•	•	•	•	
Canvasback		•	•	•	•	
Redhead		•	•	•	•	
Ring-necked Duck		•		•	•	
Greater Scaup		•	•	•	•	
Lesser Scaup		•		•	•	
Common Eider					•	
King Eider		•			•	
Steller's Eider				•		
Harlequin Duck	•	•	•	•	•	
Oldsquaw		•	•	•	•	
Black Scoter		•	•	•	•	
Surf Scoter		•	•	•	•	
White-winged Scoter		•	•	•	•	
Common Goldeneye		•	•	•	•	
Barrow's Goldeneye		•	•	•	•	
Bufflehead		•	•	•	•	
Hooded Merganser	•	•	•	•	•	
Common Merganser	•	•	•	•	•	
Red-breasted Merganser	•	•	•	•	•	
Ruddy Duck					•	
Osprey		•	•	•		
Bald Eagle	•	•	•	•	•	
Northern Harrier		•		•	•	
Sharp-shinned Hawk		•	•	•	•	
Northern Goshawk		•	•	•	•	
Red-tailed Hawk	•	•	•	•	•	

	Br	Sp	Su	Fa	Wi	
American Kestrel			•	•	•	
Merlin			•	•		
Peregrine Falcon	•	•	•	•	•	
Ring-necked Pheasant		•	•	•	•	
Blue Grouse	•	•	•	•	•	
Rock Ptarmigan		•				
Virginia Rail		•			•	
Sora		•	•	•	•	
American Coot		•		•	•	
Sandhill Crane	•	•	•	•		
Black-bellied Plover		•	•	•		
Lesser Golden-Plover		•	•	•		
Snowy Plover			•			
Semipalmated Plover	•	•	•	•		
Killdeer	•	•	•	•	•	
Black Oystercatcher	•	•	•	•	•	
Greater Yellowlegs		•	•	•	•	
Lesser Yellowlegs		•	•	•		
Solitary Sandpiper		•	•			
Wandering Tattler		•	•	•		
Spotted Sandpiper	•	•	•	•		
Upland Sandpiper			•			
Whimbrel		•	•	•		
Marbled Godwit		•				
Ruddy Turnstone		•	•	•	•	
Black Turnstone		•	•	•	•	
Surfbird		•	•	•	•	
Red Knot		•	•	•		
Sanderling		•	•	•	•	
Sempalmated Sandpiper			•			
Western Sandpiper		•	•	•		
Least Sandpiper	•	•	•	•	•	
Baird's Sandpiper		•	•	•		
Pectoral Sandpiper		•	•	•		
Sharp-tailed Sandpiper			•	•	•	
Rock Sandpiper		•		•	•	
Dunlin		•	•	•	•	
Curlew Sandpiper			•			
Buff-breasted Sandpiper			•			

	Br	Sp	Su	Fa	Wi	
Short-billed Dowitcher	•	•	•	•		
Long-billed Dowitcher		•	•	•	•	
Common Snipe	•	•	•	•	•	
Red-necked Phalarope		•	•	•		
Red Phalarope		•	•	•		
Pomarine Jaeger		•	•	•	•	
Parasitic Jaeger		•	•	•	•	
Long-tailed Jaeger		•	•	•	•	
South Polar Skua			•	•		
Franklin's Gull			•			
Bonaparte's Gull			•			
Mew Gull		•	•	•	•	
Ring-billed Gull		•	•		•	
California Gull		•	•			
Herring Gull		•	•	•	•	
Thayer's Gull		•	•		•	
Western Gull		•		•	•	
Glaucous-winged Gull	•	•	•	•	•	
Glaucous Gull		•	•		•	
Black-legged Kittiwake		•	•	•	•	
Sabine's Gull		•	•	•	•	
Caspian Tern		•	•	•		
Arctic Tern		•	•	•		
Aleutian Tern		•	•			
Common Murre	•	•	•	•	•	
Thick-billed Murre		•	•		•	
Pigeon Guillemot	•	•	•	•	•	
Marbled Murrelet	•	•	•	•	•	
Ancient Murrelet	•	•	•	•	•	
Cassin's Auklet	•	•	•	•		
Rhinoceros Auklet	•	•	•	•	•	
Tufted Puffin	•	•	•	•		
Horned Puffin	•	•	•	•	•	
Rock Dove		•	•	•	•	
Band-tailed Pigeon			•	•		
Mourning Dove			•	•		
Great Horned Owl		•				
Snowy Owl				•	•	
Long-eared Owl				•		

	Br	Sp	Su	Fa	Wi	
Short-eared Owl			•	•		
Northern Saw-whet Owl	•	•	•	•	•	
Common Nighthawk				•		
Rufous Hummingbird	•	•	•	•		
Belted Kingfisher	•	•	•	•	•	
Lewis' Woodpecker				•		
Red-breasted Sapsucker	•	•	•	•	•	
Downy Woodpecker		•	•			
Hairy Woodpecker	•	•	•	•	•	
Northern Flicker	•	•	•	•	•	
Western Flycatcher	•	•	•	•		
Eastern Kingbird		•	•			
Horned Lark		•		•		
Tree Swallow	•	•	•			
Violet-green Swallow		•	•	•		
Cliff Swallow			•			
Barn Swallow	•	•	•	•		
Steller's Jay	•	•	•	•	•	
Clark's Nutcracker				•	•	
Northwestern Crow	•	•	•	•	•	
Common Raven	•	•	•	•	•	
Chestnut-backed Chickadee	•	•	•	•	•	
Red-breasted Nuthatch	•	•	•	•	•	
Brown Creeper	•	•	•	•	•	
House Wren				•		
Winter Wren	•	•	•	•	•	
American Dipper	•	•	•	•	•	
Golden-crowned Kinglet	•	•	•	•	•	
Ruby-crowned Kinglet		•	•	•		
Mountain Bluebird				•		
Townsend's Solitaire				•	•	
Swainson's Thrush	•	•	•			
Hermit Thrush	•	•	•		•	
American Robin	•	•	•	•	•	
Varied Thrush	•	•	•	•	•	
Water Pipit		•	•	•	•	
Bohemian Waxwing			•	•	•	
Cedar Waxwing			•	•	•	

	Br	Sp	Su	Fa	Wi	
Northern Shrike		•		•	•	
European Starling	•	•	•	•	•	
Orange-crowned Warbler	•	•	•	•	•	
Yellow-rumped Warbler		•		•	•	
Townsend's Warbler	•	•	•	•		
Wilson's Warbler	•	•	•	•		
American Tree Sparrow				•	•	
Chipping Sparrow			•		•	
Savannah Sparrow		•	•	•	•	
Fox Sparrow	•	•	•	•	•	
Song Sparrow	•	•	•	•	•	
Lincoln's Sparrow	•	•	•	•	•	
White-throated Sparrow					•	
Golden-crowned Sparrow		•		•	•	
White-crowned Sparrow		•		•	•	
Dark-eyed Junco	•	•	•	•	•	
Lapland Longspur				•	•	
Snow Bunting			•	•	•	
Red-winged Blackbird		•	•	•	•	
Western Meadowlark				•		
Brewer's Blackbird		•	•	•	•	
Boat-tailed Grackle				•		
Brown-headed Cowbird		•	•	•		
Brambling		•		•		
Pine Grosbeak	•	•	•	•	•	
Red Crossbill	•	•	•	•	•	
White-winged Crossbill		•	•			
Common Redpoll				•	•	
Pine Siskin	•	•	•	•	•	
American Goldfinch			•			
Evening Grosbeak				•		

* Records from Birds of B.C. Vol. 1 & the Royal B.C. Museum

191

MARINE MAMMALS AND REPTILES OF THE QUEEN CHARLOTTE ISLANDS *			
REPTILES	**Nearshore**	**Offshore**	
Leatherback (marine turtle)		•	
MAMMALS			
Sea Otter	•		
Northern Fur Seal	•		
Steller Sea Lion	•		
California Sea Lion	•		
Northern Elephant Seal	•		
Harbour Seal	•		
Black Right Whale		•	
Minke Whale	•		
Sei Whale		•	
Blue Whale		•	
Fin Whale		•	
Humpback Whale	•		
Short-finned Pilot Whale	•		
Risso's Dolphin		•	
Pacific White-sided Dolphin	•		
Killer Whale	•		
Gray Whale	•		
Harbour Porpoise	•		
Dall's Porpoise	•		
Sperm Whale		•	
North Pacific Bottle-nosed Whale		•	
Bering Sea Beaked Whale		•	
Goose-beaked Whale		•	

* Based on records from the Royal British Columbia Museum

LAND MAMMALS AND AMPHIBIANS OF THE QUEEN CHARLOTTE ISLANDS *				
AMPHIBIANS	**Native**	**Introduced**	**Extinct**	
Western Toad	•			
Pacific Treefrog		1960's		
MAMMALS				
Dusky Shrew	•			
Silver-haired Bat	•			
California Myotis (bat)	•			
Keen's Myotis (bat)	•			
Long-eared Myotis (bat)	•			
Little Brown Myotis (bat)	•			
Muskrat		1925		
Beaver		1936, 1950		
Deer Mouse	•			
House Mouse		Date unknown		
Norway Rat		Date unknown		
Black Rat		Date unknown		
Red Squirrel		1950		
River Otter	•			
Marten	•			
Ermine (weasel)	•			
Raccoon		1940's		
Black Bear	•			
Red Deer		1911 , 1912	•	
Elk		1931 - 32		
Mule Deer (Sitka Deer)		1901 , 1925		
Dawson Caribou	•		•	
* Based on records from the Royal British Columbia Museum				

About the Authors

Dennis Horwood

Dennis Horwood's love of nature took him to Yoho National Park on British Columbia's Great Divide. He worked there as a naturalist for several years. In 1979 he moved to Kitimat on B.C.'s north coast, where he continues to teach elementary science. He and Tom Parkin knew one another during their days in the Rockies, but subsequently lost contact. A chance meeting seven years later re-established the friendship which ultimately produced this guide. An avid birder, Dennis has provided the Royal British Columbia Museum with many local records. As a volunteer Ecological Reserves Warden, he monitors three reserves in the northwest. His articles and photographs about wildife have appeared in numerous books, magazines, and papers. A boating enthusiast and marine naturalist, he spends each summer investigating B.C. waters with his wife Brenda and their children Andrew, Philip, and Jennifer.

Tom Parkin

After graduation from U.B.C. in 1974, Tom Parkin had a ten year career with the national and provincial parks of western Canada. For several of these years he was Manager of Visitor Services for all northwestern B.C. provincial parks. He and his wife MaryAnn now enjoy life in Nanaimo on Vancouver Island. Since 1981 Tom has been a full-time outdoor writer and photographer, and serves as Field Editor with *Explore* magazine and *Milepost* travel guide. His work has appeared in numerous magazines and books across Canada and the U.S. Editors of the second edition of *The Canadian Encyclopedia* included him among "Canada's foremost contemporary photographers." He has won major awards for photography, and has been honored by peers from the Outdoor Writers of Canada.

Index

Field Notes